Praise

"Born in Baltimore and raised in the neighborhood where Freddie Gray died while in police custody, I've known, worked with, and demonstrated alongside of Willa Bickham and Brendan Walsh. Their book helps us to understand how they've managed to keep their faith with a soup ladle in one hand and a picket sign in the other. Suffice it to say, as bad as too many parts of Baltimore are becoming, things would be even worse if two lonely drum majors for justice and peace had not been here. Thank God (or Deo Gratias as Dorothy Day's gravestone exclaims) they are with us, and their book too."

—Ralph E. Moore, Jr., long time Baltimore activist and brother in many struggles

"What a joy to have such a beautiful piece of Baltimore to share! How can stories full of heartbreak also brim with hope? It helps to be in the company of such amazing watercolors. But who can be surprised if it comes from Willa and Brendan? This lovely book is a window, not just into their lives for nearly five decades, but also their ever-generous hearts dedicated to those they have loved in their work on Mount St. Thank God for their steadfast faith in "building a society where it is easier to be good." And thanks to them for this extra labor of love we can all take home!"

—Joanne Kennedy, managing editor of *The Catholic Worker*

"Thanks from the heart for 48 stupendous years. And now a book to mark the work. Journalism with heart and mind – so rare. The poor, neglected there or here, honored with anecdote and art. You bless us all. A light to walk by in such savage times."

—Daniel Berrigan, S.J., priest, poet, teacher, resister

"I am rejoicing in this book Willa and Brendan have birthed. It tells an amazing story, and this is a story that needs telling. It needs telling especially now. It needs telling especially in this country with its endless wars. It is impossible to disengage the military from poverty. It needs telling especially in Baltimore, because Baltimore is a city that is profoundly ruptured by economic and racial conflict. And, try, as the politicians and the press might, it is impossible to disengage the economic from racial elements. Willa and Brendan know this intimately; they live smack dab in the midst of the poverty, the drug trade, and all the violence that goes with it.

Brendan is able, in the context of so much death and killing in Baltimore, to explain that the selling of drugs is the core economy in Southwest Baltimore and in too many communities all over this country. Willa's art, aside from being stunningly beautiful, is consistently the outpouring of her compassion with the people around her. And it is often, if not always, a creation in collaboration with Brendan."

—Elizabeth McAlister, co-founder Jonah House, Baltimore; resister, artist

"This volume is one of real christian art. And real christian words. And this is the beauty that comes from lives spent in service of real christian ideals in a very real and unchristian place called Baltimore, Maryland."

—David Simon, writer, film-maker, truth-teller

"In *The Long Loneliness* in Baltimore, Brendan Walsh and Willa Bickham engage in the hallowed and holy enterprise of bearing witness. In the narrative of Viva House's half-century presence in blighted Southwest Baltimore, in the catalogue of saints who have passed through the neighboring streets and the doors of their home, and in the stories attesting to the lives, the courage, and the wisdom encountered in ordinary people, we are brought face to face with the poor. They are no longer invisible. Brendan's unflinching narrative and Willa's delicately rendered illustrations of daily life in a merciless city that has abandoned its most vulnerable citizens, gives a face and a name to the anonymous poor. Wonderfully, what we find in this testament of faith is not so much poverty as vast richness. I lived in Baltimore for nearly two decades, and thought I knew my city well---but Brendan and Willa's book has further opened my eyes to her fractured beauty and her hidden grace."

—Angela Alaimo O'Donnell, poet, editor, professor, Fordham University

THE LONG LONELINESS IN BALTIMORE

Stories Along the Way

Text by Brendan Walsh
Artwork by Willa Bickham

THE LONG LONELINESS
IN BALTIMORE

Stories Along the Way

Text by Brendan Walsh
Artwork by Willa Bickham

Apprentice House
Loyola University Maryland
Baltimore, Maryland

First Edition

Printed in the United States of America

Hardcover ISBN: 978-1-62720-120-9

Design: Jacqueline Kovach
Editorial Development: Ellen Roussel, Alexandra Maule

Published by Apprentice House

Apprentice House
Loyola University Maryland
4501 N. Charles Street
Baltimore, MD 21210
410.617.5265 • 410.617.2198 (fax)
www.ApprenticeHouse.com
info@ApprenticeHouse.com

To the Walsh-Little Family

Our daughter, Kate
her husband, Dave
and
three loving granddaughters,
Maya, Grace, and Julia

They have lived with us
and continue to work with us.
They breathe life and joy into Viva House
with their lives.

Contents

Art

Seed hope
Flower Peace

—Dan Berrigan, S.J.

—Viva House, Catholic Worker
Baltimore
2007

The temple stands unfinished until all are housed in dignity.

for Viva House, Baltimore Catholic Worker, 2006

Preface

FATHER DES WILSON

The immense enthusiasm of the earliest Christians, Peter, John, Paul, and thousands more, propelled them out of hiding and on to the streets to convert the world. They carried a message from a teacher who, they were sure, was both divinely enlightened and literally down to earth. But when their enthusiasm met with other people's indifference, they saw how awful their world could be, and their enthusiasm received a sad blow. What they promised was wonderful, but most people thought the cost of achieving it would be more than they were prepared to spend.

In the Athens marketplace people who listened courteously to Paul, the intellectual from Tarsus, said, "This is all most interesting, Paul, no doubt we can hear from you about it—some other time." Then he realised that the biggest obstacle to his divine message was not that the messenger might be killed but that the message would be deemed unsuitable for the marketplace.

The marketplace in Athens decided what was practical and profitable, just as market forces calculate and decide the same today. As he licked the spiritual wounds of his rejection, Paul, who believed such a spiritually unambitious world must end soon, could not have imagined that market forces for the next two thousand years would go on deciding whether the divine message would even be heard.

An extraordinary thing happened to the Christians. They divided not only into factions but also into power groups. The world had to be changed. Many people admitted that, but how? Would it be the way of the Pharisees, restating the old rules for a good life and following them rigidly? Or would it be to see the world as an enemy and flee for your life into caves and deserts, become perfect yourself, and pray for a world you cannot convert face to face? For some Christians, it became a matter of taking hold of government and commanding the people into the good life. For others, it was a matter of becoming perfect oneself so that others might be encouraged to do the same.

But others, precious others, recognised a vital divine message that saved them from choosing either to dominate others or to efface themselves. If you want to find life's divine meaning, go to the multitudes, the people, the crowded places where God's people are, because that's where the founder of Christianity presented it to the world in the first place.

There is a saying, "If you go on pilgrimage to Rome looking for the Lord, better bring the Lord along with you." Which is another way of saying if you want to find and share the divine presence in this world, don't go away, stay around. The Kingdom of God is in you and around you, as long as God's people are around you.

Francis of Assisi and Dorothy Day and Peter Maurin looked to see if their God was to be found in a marketplace of shiny goods. They found their God in people who had no shiny goods to offer. And they found two great tasks that turned out to be privileges: the first, to announce to the world the dignity of God's people; and the second, to enhance the life of soul, body, and mind and turn their mourning into joy.

It is not an easy life, as our friends at Viva House know from their own experience and that of their neighbors. There are so many obstacles in a world where death is said to be a solution to our problems, where wealth and beauty are for the few, and where the sorrow of fellow creatures can be public policy because that's what the marketplace requires. This means that some people have to pull and haul, some have to wait around hungry until called for, some have to beg for what's left over. Still others find great bargains when another's stall collapses. In this world safety is said to be assured by war and the penalty of death.

In that worldly marketplace, the followers of Dorothy Day, Peter Maurin, and the saints coming after them have been the guardians of our souls for many, many years and will go on being so for many years to come. We are grateful to them. Grateful for their message of human dignity recognised, all life enhanced. Grateful for the message that human dignity needs and will receive more than alms. It will receive generosity that can be repaid but cannot be repaid in full, because every act of divine generosity is a unique gift we give to each other.

When we feel despondent about a world that tells us to be proud of selfishness, we reflect on half a century of giving, feeding, sheltering, protecting, and sharing the divine vision that has been the spiritual life of Viva House in Baltimore.

We found faithful friends here to enrich our own troubled lives in Ireland too, and we are grateful for such a blessing.

As long as your voice is still to be heard, our hopes are still alive, even in the marketplace.

Viva House has been a friend of Fr. Des Wilson since the late 1980s. Des has been living in West Belfast since 1966. In 1975 he was assigned to Ballmurphy, one of the most impoverished and vilified areas of the city. He has drawn inspiration from the community around him. During the war years, 1968-1998, known as The Troubles, people in Ballymurphy created and developed their own responses to the political, social, and economic crises they faced. Des is often referred to as the "people's priest."

Modern society calls the **beggars** bums and panhandlers and give's them the bum's rush.

But the Greeks used to say that **people in need** are, in fact, the **ambassadors** of the **gods.**

-Peter Maurin

Foreword

DAVID SIMON

"Glorious years. Hard times."

In the prose that accompanies this compendium of Willa Bickham's deep and artistic affirmations of moral resistance and human liberation, her husband, Brendan Walsh, offers those two descriptive fragments in rapid succession, one hard on the heels of the other.

If you know Bickham and Walsh, if you know their deep commitment to Viva House, to the people served by that outpost of compassion and civility, and certainly if you know something of life in West Baltimore, you understand that the words purpose no contradiction at all.

Quoting one of my few remaining heroes, the great independent journalist and thinker I. F. Stone, Walsh further acknowledges the joy of rightful struggle and the deep insight of Stone's claim that often the only battles worth fighting are the ones you know you are going to lose.

"Yes, we have lost most of the battles, but there is a measure of truthfulness when you try to give a human face to those who suffer," writes Walsh. "There is hope when you actually name the evil and do your best to confront it."

Here, Walsh is self-effacing to a flaw: It is more than a measure of truthfulness. It is the full measure. For four decades, Walsh and Bickham have committed to replenishing the reservoir of empathy and human dignity that often threatens to run dry on the corners of Mount or Monroe or Fayette streets or on Fulton or Edmondson avenues. That is an adult lifetime spent in quotidian observance of the simple and abiding premise that all of us matter, that we are all of us sacred, and that any system of governance or economics that can produce this much wasted human potential is an affront to the human spirit.

The problems that they have faced every day at Viva House and in their daily traverse of the community that they call home have proved unrelenting. And yet Brendan and Willa are, in the last analysis, equally relentless.

They have not wavered. Their love for their neighbors, for their community, and for their city—my city, our city—has not been eroded by years of systemic unemployment, homelessness, hunger, brutality, and astonishing societal indifference. I have known them for years. They are unyielding in their capacity to hope. And among all the various currencies that modern America has used to measure progress and failure, success and stagnation, hope is perhaps the only gathered treasure of which even the most vulnerable can still gather and bank and spend. Hope is the elemental origin of all that is or can become good.

In looking at this collection of Willa Bickham's political and humanistic art—some of it pleading, some of it angry, and all of it so deeply purposed—I am taken especially by the fact that it offers no scent of the presumed innocence that the more cynical among us usually ascribe to so-called moralists and do-gooders. It has become fashionable over the last three-and-a-half decades to mock and belittle the naïveté of those among us who commit their lives to deep and abiding human service or who would dare to make any argument against the notion that capitalist markets are the fixed and inevitable arbiters of what has value and merit in this world. We live in a world in which capital has won all the battles, and the presumption is that every solution to every problem must now and henceforth get the money right first. Those that measure life in other terms are increasingly a source of pity, if not comedy, to those riding atop this great monied wave.

It has been so for a long time now.

An American president took office thirty-five years ago and declared—with all the cheap and facile insight that an amoral ideology so handily offers—that America had fought a war on poverty and poverty had won. And in so arguing for this abject surrender to systemic dehumanization, that still-revered president was thought clever, if not downright sagacious.

And since that ugly premise was first openly voiced, the abandonment of places like West Baltimore, North Philadelphia, East St. Louis, and South Chicago has become endemic to our political culture. Entire election cycles rush by without a mention of the poor or homelessness or hunger or mass incarceration.

Nothing of what is witnessed every day at Viva House and in the communities it serves allows for such willful silence, and the reality of what Willa Bickham and Brendan Walsh confront every day steels their words and art against any cynical claims of innocence or sentiment.

"Love without wisdom and courage is sentimentality, as with the ordinary church member," writes Walsh, quoting the pacifist Ammon Hennacy. "Wisdom without love and courage is cowardice, as with the ordinary intellectual. Courage without love and wisdom is foolhardiness, as with the ordinary soldier."

The life that Brendan Walsh and Willa Bickham have fashioned for themselves on South Mount Street—and the good works of their life's creation, Viva House, among the people of Southwest Baltimore—is anything but ordinary. And their gathered insight is anything but ordinary.

I first met them as a newspaper reporter perhaps a quarter century ago, gathering a few facts here and there for some daily coverage of no lasting consequence. Their warm yet blunt assessment of the civic realities was refreshing and helpful, to be sure. But I don't think the great arc of their personal journey was entirely revealed to me. I left Mount Street with my handful of facts and quotes; they remained there, day after day, to serve those meals and rally to the side of their neighbors and to argue for something better.

But in 1993, while following some of the most vulnerable Baltimoreans through their daily travails for a book on the bloated diaspora of addiction and the ravages of the drug war, I found myself time and again on South Mount Street, in the company of people living moment to moment and meal to meal. I found myself at the Viva House lunch tables in the company of Gary McCullough or Ronnie Boice or any number of others for whom existence was spinning beyond all control.

And there on the walls of the dining room, I encountered some of Willa Bickham's aphoristic and water-colored art. But no platitude need apply within those silk screens and posters. Not at all. There is comfort in Willa's work, and many of the images in this volume offer great warmth and encouragement, but there is, as well, an argument to be heard.

In some of the most affecting pieces, the art itself is soft and affecting, but the quotes that accompany those images are firm and assured. They come from Behan and Berrigan, from Jeremiah and Langston Hughes, and from the women of the Weather Underground.

"I respect justice to human beings first of all," declares the great Irish playwright and provocateur Brendan Behan against a Christmas silk-screen of a contemplative and pregnant woman. "I have a total irreverence for anything connected with society except that which makes the roads safer, the beer stronger, the food cheaper, and old folks and children warmer in the winter and happier in the summer."

Or Peter Maurin's words against Bickham's imagery of the bundled homeless in the Baltimore snow: "Modern society calls the beggars bums and panhandlers and gives them the bum's rush, but the Greeks used to say that people in need are, in fact, the ambassadors of the gods."

Or Willa's cover of a Baltimore-produced magazine of women's liberation, featuring a Matisse-like papier-image of a female form caught between two dark monolithic shapes, her mouth open to the heavens: "If a woman is hurtin', don't tell her how to holler."

Among those whom I followed into Viva House for free meals and respite in that strange, lost year of immersion journalism, Gary McCullough was in many respects the heart of the book that would become *The Corner: A Year in the Life of An Inner-City Neighborhood*. And regardless of the heroin haze in which he frequently hid from the world, Gary could not help but be engaged on any and every human or intellectual level. Time and again, I would be pulled up by my presumptions and stereotypes about addiction, about race, about class by this warm, damaged soul for whom there was never even poison to narcotize himself from the human condition. Gary McCullough loved people and he loved the world, even if that world didn't always love him.

The last word here will go to him.

The year that I came to know him, Gary McCullough read Karen Armstrong's *History of God* and debated monotheistic philosophies in his mother's basement; he made himself the best summer employee that the Pratt Street crab houses had ever seen; and when the weather turned and the money was no longer there for his addiction, much less for food, he leaned hard on Viva House to provide. And then, his belly full for a long moment, he would wander the dining rooms, admiring Willa's imagery and the words of so many socialists and writers and saints.

And once, walking back onto Mount Street after being so revived, Gary pulled me up with a remark as earnest as it was precise.

"Those people are Christians."

"They are," I agreed, and I began to explain the specific and technical status of Viva House with regard to the Catholic Worker Community.

Gary shook his head at me. I didn't understand.

"I'm not talking about no church," he said. "I'm talking about christians."

I was slow to understand.

"Little 'c'. Lower-case 'c'," Gary said finally. "Not no church. They're really, actually christian up in there."

And suddenly, I understood.

I am a Jew myself and a largely secular one at that. And like Gary, I too am wary of the very label of any religionist, particularly those who enjoy an organized and structured faith that is so firmly entrenched in the social and political framework of this too-broken, too-monied, and too-pleasured country. Without even verbalizing it, I think I had long held most self-professed Catholics and Lutherans and Methodists and Episcopalians to be suspect and complicit in any number of human failures and hypocrisies. Yet until that day on Mount Street with Gary McCullough, I had not even said the words aloud, much less formed a clear thought about the matter. But yes, I didn't really trust the word Christian.

"They're christians." he said again. "Real christians."

And I understood him entirely.

This volume is one of real christian art. And real christian words.

And this is the beauty that comes from lives spent in service of real christian ideals in a very real and unchristian place called Baltimore, Maryland.

Gary McCullough would have loved this book. I miss him hard.

David Simon is an award-winning journalist and writer. Most people know David Simon through his masterpieces, Homicide: Life on the Streets, The Corner, and The Wire among his television works. Viva House knows him because he truly understands both the systemic and individualistic causes of poverty and violence. David Simon tells the truth.

I Stuck my head out of the
window this Morning and
SPRING
Kissed
Me bang in the face.

—Willa

—Langston Hughes

Let us
sit down
soon to eat
with all those who
have not eaten.
Let us set tables
with strawberries
in the snow
and a plate
like the moon
itself from which
all can eat.
For now, I ask
no more than the
Justice
of
eating.

—Pablo Neruda

Introduction

WILLA BICKHAM & BRENDAN WALSH

"We have all known the long loneliness and we have learned that the only solution is love and that love comes with community."
—Dorothy Day

Loneliness. Love. Community. For almost a half century, workers at Viva House have grappled with Dorothy Day's understanding of loneliness and more importantly, her "only solution," love. The title of this book is meant to honor Dorothy Day and to share in her understanding of loneliness.

The loneliness we have encountered in the Viva House neighborhood, zip code 21223, Baltimore, Maryland, known as Sowebo (Southwest Baltimore), has brought us to our knees. Literally.

The loneliness appears in multiple forms. Murders are a frequent occurrence. Since 1968, almost twelve thousand people have been murdered in Baltimore, three times the number killed in the six occupied counties of the North of Ireland during the war years, 1968– 1998. Four people have been shot and killed on our block alone, two very close to our front door.

Open air drug markets, the essence of Sowebo's economy, operate freely. The authorities are powerless to stop the drug trade, and quite often the police merely add to the violence of the situation. Evictions, "abando-miniums," deaths by freezing, deaths by house fire, and housing code violations are all part of everyday life in Sowebo. There is nothing lonelier than an evicted family, an addict without community, or people merely eking out an existence. Ask anyone sleeping rough,"What is the hardest thing? The cold? The hunger?" "No, it's the loneliness! You become invisible."

Between 1950 and 2015, Baltimore lost one-third of its population and at least 150,000 solid blue collar jobs. These jobs were replaced by low paid, nonunion work, and 25 percent of the city's population exists below poverty level. The stark reality is that many, many people will become a permanent underclass. They will never earn a just, family-supporting wage. Many see themselves as expendable people.

We never believed that loneliness should have the last word. There is a simple solution. We believe in the common good. No one is entitled to more than he or she needs while others lack necessities. We believe in community and justice. We believe in doing the works of mercy and resisting the works of war and violence. We believe in love, the only solution. So Viva House is a simple Catholic Worker (CW) house of hospitality and resistance. During the first forty-five years, more than a million people have come to our door seeking food, financial assistance, shelter, or just a place to meet and talk. And we have engaged in numerous acts of resistance to all the dirty wars our country has waged, Vietnam through Iraq and Afghanistan. Endless wars now embrace unending poverty. And we have resisted all the sleazy deals developers and bankers have forced upon Baltimore City. Mostly the rich got more than they needed, and the poor have been sent away empty.

This book is a compilation of reflections about what we have seen and heard for five decades, drawn from our newsletter, Enthusiasm. Chapter 1 was written specifically for this volume. Throughout we attempt to explain our work through graphic art, poetry, parables, and essays, snapshots of a life we have experienced. We hope it offers some hope, especially for the seemingly powerless who are continually mocked by the powerful.

A single act of Kindness throws out roots in all directions and the roots spring up and make new trees.

—Amelia Earhart

3

PROBLEMS STEM FROM OUR ACCEPTANCE of this FILTHY ROTTEN SYSTEM

— Dorothy Day
The Catholic Worker

4

Chapter 1: Viva!

Rejoice with us! After painful months, decisions, and no decisions, we have finally located a house and have begun. We have chosen to name our home Viva House. There could be no other name. Life is sacred; its alternative is death. We think of life especially at this time while we await the birth of our daughter, Kate.
—Viva House newsletter, September 1968

Little by Little: Enormous Ideas, Small House: 1968

These words were part of our first news and appeal letter. We mailed it in September 1968 to approximately one hundred people. Dorothy Day printed the letter in the November 1968 issue of the New York *Catholic Worker*. We've been doing the work now for almost a half century. When things went well, the years zoomed by. When life was more difficult and challenging, time was more of a heavy burden.

When we opened Viva House in October 1968, we never imagined that we would still be doing this work a half century later. Over the years, we have embraced many people, witnessed what the eyes should and should not see, heard songs of celebration and the anguished cries of people who suffer, and touched the beauty and misery of life.

Often people asked, "What have you done for almost fifty years?" There is a simple reply that usually satisfies the media and bean counters. We provided more than one million meals for people; served as a temporary home to over three thousand women, children, and men; and distributed over 375 tons of food to neighborhood families (or more accurately, returned stolen goods to them). We keep accurate records just to be sure we have enough food for meals and food bags.

But it is our hope that we accomplished more than these deeds. We tried to adhere to the spirituality and philosophy of the Catholic Worker. We endeavored to make Viva House a sacred place, a place dedicated to people, a place where weary people could rest and gain strength. We tried to be neighbor, not agency. Additionally, Viva House has been a place for discussion and clarification of local, national, and international issues. It has been a gathering place where people talked seriously and made plans for acts of nonviolent resistance to the greed and violence so peculiar to United States culture. It has become clear to us that we are a nation in love with death. We worship it. Embrace it. And we are devoured by it.

In Ireland they say it is necessary to fight both the famine *and* the crown simultaneously. Which is to say, it is necessary that we serve as a house of hospitality *and* resistance. It is a huge task. The ideas and goals are enormous. Our house is small. We do what we can. Our success has not been, and probably will not be, a victory over violence and greed. The Catholic Worker movement believes that success, as the world determines it, is not the criterion by which a movement should be judged. The most important thing is that we do the works of mercy and resist the works of war.

Baptized into the Fire and Blessed: 1968–1980

In 1967, when Willa and I first met in Baltimore, we realized immediately that we were soul mates. Our backgrounds were similar. Willa had been a nun in Chicago, and I had been a seminarian in New York City.

We also realized that we were both opposed to the Vietnam War and wanted to live and work among people who lived in poverty. And, most importantly, we loved one another and married in December 1967, less than six months after we first met. How about that!

Willa and I were enthused by the example of Dorothy Day and the clear vision of the Catholic Worker movement. Catholic Workers were national leaders in nonviolent resistance to the military draft and the war in Vietnam. They also lived among the poor, served meals to the hungry, and provided housing for the homeless. We wanted to be part of this movement.

So, eight months after our wedding, we began Viva House. It was that simple. How about that!

We located what became Viva House on August 26, 1968. It was a typical summer day in Baltimore—hazy, hot, and humid—and we stepped into Lou and Sarah Eisenberg's neighborhood grocery store in the 1800 block of West Lombard Street. While slurping snowballs, we inquired about the House for Rent sign hanging in the storefront window. The house was a three-story, ten-room, two-bath row house in the unit block of South Mount Street. The rent was seventy-five dollars per month plus all utilities except water and sewer charges. It was in rough, rat-infested condition and had been abandoned for at least a year. The basic systems—furnace, electric, gas, and plumbing— were in usable shape and we agreed to rent immediately. Dorothy Day asked Pat Rusk and Andy Chrusciel, members of the New York Catholic Worker, to help us get the house in shape. A beautiful gift.

From 1968 until 1975 we rented Viva House. The rent never increased. Repairs were always completed as needed. The Eisenbergs, our landlords, were always fair and generous with us, and in 1975 they sold us the house for one thousand dollars. Indeed, we have been fortunate.

After a month of plastering, scrubbing, painting, and evicting rats and roaches, we opened the house for guests in October 1968. The first arrivals were members of the Catonsville Nine, seven men and two women who had burned 1-A draft files taken from the Selective Service office in Catonsville, Maryland. Many of the nine stayed at the house, where they were able to prepare for trial with attorneys William Kunstler, Harold Buckman, and Bill Cunningham, S.J. For two weeks before the trial, the house was filled with people day and night. We were delighted to have Dorothy Day with us for the trial. The house was so hectic that St. Martin's Convent nearby graciously provided a room for Dorothy, then seventy years old, to rest. We were off to an energetic beginning. The trial and Dorothy's presence fortified us and gave us a clear sense of direction. Viva House was baptized into the fire and blessed.

After the trial, our neighbor Nicole Dorsett and her newborn son, Michael, moved in. They stayed with us for about eight months and helped immeasurably with hospitality. We are indebted to Nicole for her great support when our daughter, Kate, was born in 1969. During 1969, we provided temporary housing for about thirty-five single men and had an open table at dinner time. Almost all the men were over the age of fifty, and many were permanently disabled. For the most part the house was calm and peaceful. I had been ordered to do alternative service as a conscientious objector to the Vietnam War and worked in the psychiatric unit of Johns Hopkins Hospital for two years. During my second year, I worked the night shift. This made me more available during the day, but it also left Willa and Kate alone at night, often in a house filled with men.

Obviously, we had a tremendous trust in Divine Providence. Still, we had a particularly sobering incident. One of our guests, a man fighting drug addiction, collected the house television, toaster, blender, and radio and walked out the front door before dawn. Many of the items were wedding gifts and were missed. But the real problem was the violence that accompanied the theft. Another guest, a man suffering from severe lung congestion, could not climb steps and slept on the first floor near the front door. The addicted man threatened him with a knife if he made the slightest sound. We shudder to think what might have happened. After that, we were no longer naïve Catholic Workers.

When our daughter, Kate, was born, the house became a real home, and we developed stronger solidarity with our neighbors. Viva House was the second from the end of a row of attached houses. On one side was a family with six children; on the other side, four apartments always housed at least three children among them. So, "wee wanes" were constantly in and out of Viva House. More than anything else, children humanize all situations and make life whole and holy.

The number of people coming for our dinner meal at the open table had grown steadily, and we thought a storefront would be ideal to accommodate the increasing number. So, just before Christmas 1969, we opened a storefront kitchen five blocks from the house.

Initially, Mary Brawley came from the New York Catholic Worker to help us begin the storefront. Then Viva House evolved into a sizeable live-in community. Our friends Jim Lyko, Joe Lynch, Frank Kasper, Chris Cotter, and John Hogan all lived and worked with us at the house during the storefront years. The storefront was open five days each week from 8 a.m. until 1 p.m. We had social time for the first three hours and then served huge pots of soup and mounds of bread during the last two hours. Tom Lewis, one of the Catonsville Nine, introduced us to his parents, Al and Pauline. They were a godsend. Al, who had worked for Nabisco, kept us stocked with Nabisco goodies, and Pauline prepared chicken stew weekly. Anne and Frank Brusca of the Anawim Community kept us supplied with love, ideas, and food. In addition to the meals, we provided other services. We collected clean, used clothing for distribution to those in need of a warm coat, a new pair of pants, a sweater, or shoes. Jim Lyko cut hair. Joe Lynch and our neighbor, Mary Jane Bush, kept the kitchen and clothing room in smooth working order. It was a grand time!

During those early years, the Vietnam War was raging. We worked closely with Baltimore's Peace Action Center to oppose the war. The house also served as a planning site for many draft board raids. It seemed as if there was always someone here from the Milwaukee 14, the East Coast Conspiracy to Save Lives, the Dow Chemical Nine, the Chicago 15, the Camden 28, or Women against Daddy Warbucks. The FBI was also a frequent visitor. FBI agents harassed our neighbors and were always looking for someone, particularly Dan Berrigan and Mary Moylan, members of the Catonsville Nine who had gone underground. Eventually, they arrested Dan, who continually embarrassed them. Before they caught up with him, he had made numerous public appearances, including preaching a homily in church on a Sunday morning. The feds never located Mary. She turned herself in after several years in the underground.

Those first four years were a roller coaster ride. We are forever grateful for the love and support of Marilyn and Bill O'Connor, two of the first people I met when I came to Baltimore. We remember Tom Lewis, who adorned our walls with his art, and Jim Harney, who always instilled in us fresh insights into global politics. Jim was an excellent photojournalist, and he knew firsthand the freedom struggles in many countries, particularly El Salvador and Iraq. And we are indebted to Phil Berrigan, who operated the roller coaster.

Toward the end of the Vietnam War, our live-in community of resisters gradually disbanded, and we closed the storefront at the end of 1972. Our live-in community members returned to school or moved from Baltimore, but Willa and I continued to serve the meal at our house, but on a less grandiose scale. We served as many people as we could each evening.

From the very beginning, Willa and I believed that all donations to Viva House should go directly toward "the work." Thus, Willa and I worked jobs to support personal needs. During the 1970s, I taught high school, Willa went to nursing school, and Kate thrived in the local grade school. The hospitality continued. We served an average of fifteen to twenty people each evening. At the end of the month, with monthly assistance checks spent, the numbers would be higher.

We recall some fine protests during these years. The White House Pray-Ins in the summer of 1973 were quite extraordinary and included several members of our extended community. Their purpose was to demand an end to the vicious bombing campaign in Cambodia and a final conclusion to the massacre in Vietnam. The protest was quite simple. A person just joined a scheduled White House tour and, once inside the House, picked a spot and fell to their knees. There was little time for prayer, for arrests happened quickly. During the entire month of July and part of August, at least three or four people were arrested during each tour. The number arrested exceeded one hundred, and on a final day in August there was a mass arrest. It was an effective protest and kept the Cambodia bombings in the public eye. Other protests included sprinkling blood and ashes in the Pentagon on Valentine's Day 1978, and an action at the White House after the near meltdown at the Three Mile Island Nuclear Generating Station in Pennsylvania.

The most memorable events during the 1970s centered on the lack of housing for one-fourth of Baltimore's population. The problem of homelessness was growing daily. More than forty thousand families were on the waiting list for public housing. There was no rent control, and gentrification was in its formative stages. Like Columbus, those with money were "discovering" old urban neighborhoods and purchasing houses occupied by renters. They claimed them, evicted the renters, and flipped the houses, laughing all the way to the bank.

In our immediate neighborhood, gentrification appeared in the form of historic preservation. In 1970 one square block had been declared "historic." At the beginning of 1977, speculators introduced Bill 698 into the City Council. If passed, this bill would almost quadruple the boundaries of the historic district. This bill had little to do with history; it was a bank-boom bonanza. Viva House helped to organize a struggle against this bill, and members of our neighborhood were able to hold it in check for a solid year. We ultimately lost the battle, and many blocks were designated historic. Our community and our neighbors were introduced to the bitter fruit that is part of good ole U.S. capitalism. Speculators received tax breaks on their properties. Long term residents, most of whom were renters, were either moved out or forced to pay higher rents. Single Room Occupancies (SROs) disappeared, and families started to double up.

Shelter Years: 1980 – 1986

By 1980, the problem of homelessness had reached epidemic proportions. We decided to convert Viva House into a temporary shelter for homeless women and children. The existing shelter beds in Baltimore were mostly for men. There were very few places for women and children.

At first we asked our neighborhood parish, St. Martin's, to rent us its abandoned high school building for one dollar per year. We promised to raise all the renovation money necessary to convert the building into a residence for approximately fifty men, women, and children. We believed that using the space for this purpose would have helped revitalize a dying parish. Initially, the parish agreed, and it was full steam ahead. Then, "wiser episcopal heads" concluded it would be a bad idea. We made a public witness to the church's refusal but quickly moved on. There is great wisdom in Jesus' admonition, "Let the dead bury the dead."

Instead, in four short months we converted Viva House into a hospitality house for nine women and their children. For five years we were a temporary home. More than thirteen hundred women and children stayed with us. Sr. Patti Ann Rogucki, SFCC, and I coordinated the daily work of the shelter. Local supporters Courtney Petersen, Kathleen Rumpf, and Ginnie Morrow joined by members of the Jesuit Volunteers Corps brought great spirit to the work.

During the shelter years, we completed a study of homeless women in Baltimore titled *The Long Loneliness: A Study of Homeless Women in Baltimore*. It was well received by people involved in providing shelter in Baltimore. It was also helpful to the agencies and communities that were trying to determine how many women and children in Baltimore needed homes. We agitated for more public housing units and questioned the State of Maryland's policy of deinstitutionalizing the mentally ill.

The house was a home for newborn babies and a resting place for women close to death. We have great memories—women who finally got homes, women who finally got jobs, children who finally got some peace. But, the injustices have a lasting sting. Most families did not get decent homes. Most children did not live happily ever after. Most of the mentally ill wandered from shelter to shelter. For the most part, the house was a stop-off point in a revolving door.

As the years went by, it became absolutely clear that Baltimore did not have enough affordable housing to meet the huge demand of poor people. A family would be on the street; they would stay with us, accumulate two welfare checks (one for a month's security deposit, one for a month's rent), and then join the mad hunt for an overpriced piece of junk that would not pass a minimum housing code inspection. By the end of 1984, we understood that many families were doubling up in an effort to meet the rent, heat, and utility bills. Quite often the same process would be repeated, and the shelter cycle would commence once again. The revolving door was turning murderously.

In June 1983, an arsonist set fire to abandoned houses on both sides of Viva House, making the women and children living at Viva House homeless again. One of the buildings was torn down immediately, and a few years later we were able to purchase the other building by paying the back taxes.

Single women who stayed with us had usually been cast out of state hospitals. Sometimes they came in need of medication; sometimes they came with a bag of drugs. And always it was clear that these women were not benefiting from the shelter hop, from here to there to nowhere. We remember one of our guests who had shaved her head with a razor, leaving her head bleeding furiously with severe gouges. She was a fine person but desperate and afraid. She needed more than temporary shelter. She needed a long-term, loving community. When she was released from a state mental hospital in Maryland, she was offered a bus token to Baltimore, some prescriptions, and a map of possible shelters.

Most of the women and children who stayed with us were direct referrals from the Baltimore City Department of Social Services. We were becoming a branch office of city government and on the brink of institutionalization. By 1985 the waiting list for public housing was so long that an emergency waiting list had been created. To get on this list a woman had to demonstrate verifiable homelessness. Staying at a shelter was the clearest way to do this. So, women would arrive at the door and ask us to write a letter saying that they were living at Viva House. People were desperate for housing.

At the same time, we were awash with paperwork. The homeless problem was becoming the homeless business replete with structures, institutions, and bureaucracies. You had the shelter business, the health care business, the secondary shelter business—everything but affordable, decent, permanent housing. In addition, since the women who stayed with us came from every area of the city and beyond, we began losing vital contact with our own neighborhood. By the end of the 1980s, the drug war had really heated up and then raged out of control. The atmosphere during all of the 1990s was downright frightening. Sowebo was a battleground.

In 1986, we held a day-long meeting with all of the Viva House volunteers. We decided to get out of the shelter business. We pulled the plug on the merry-go-round and returned to the simple hospitality of our food pantry and soup kitchen to serve our neighbors who were without food. No more social workers. No more forms. No more questions. No more agencies.

During the shelter years, we also continued the resistance. In 1983 we celebrated the anniversary of Dorothy Day's birth by gluing truthful words on top of fallout shelter signs on various buildings in the downtown area. We chose the George Fallon Federal Building; the Catholic Center, headquarters of the Baltimore Archdiocese; and the Clarence M. Mitchell, Jr. Court House. It was a simple deed. All we needed were a ladder, strong glue, and our new fallout shelter sign. The new sign read: "Nuclear War: No Shelter! No Escape . . . Nuclear War has no cure. It can only be prevented." We had great visibility and attracted significant attention. Strangely, no one was arrested. Not even at the Catholic Center. Phil Berrigan was with us as we plodded through downtown. At the Basilica of the Assumption, Phil glued our sign over the fallout shelter sign. One of the Basilica caretakers asked him: "How would you like it if someone put this sign on your house?" Phil responded that his home, Jonah House, already had the sign in the window!

One of our most elaborate demonstrations took place in front of Baltimore City Hall a week before Christmas 1984, while then mayor William Donald Schaefer was hosting a holiday open house. We played out an urban nativity scene depicting *A Tale of Two Baltimores.* Tara, one of the women living at Viva House, and her three-week-old daughter, Megan, acted out the scene. Mother and daughter crouched in a cardboard box to represent the real Baltimore. Two people dressed in evening wear portrayed the mayor's Tinsel Town. We had wise people bearing gifts of food, clothing, homes, and meaningful work. Our inner city choir reworked Christmas carols with appropriate messages. The cast included more than one hundred people. The mayor and party goers were not pleased with our creativity.

During the shelter years, several members of our community were arrested at the White House and at the U.S. Capitol as we joined in protests against President Ronald Reagan's budget cuts organized by Washington, D.C.'s Community for Creative Nonviolence. Several of us were also arrested in Baltimore protesting military aid both to the counterrevolutionary Contras in Nicaragua and the military government in El Salvador. The community was also heavily involved in protests aimed at Johns Hopkins University's Applied Physics Laboratory. At least 90 percent of the lab's work is war-related, and much of that is nuclear.

Tireless Energy, Loving Community: 1987–present

In 1986, after shutting down the shelter, we decided to once again open an expanded soup kitchen and food pantry. After more than a year of negotiation, we purchased the building on our left side, and an anonymous donor paid for the entire rehab. The building was abandoned and in bombed-out condition. The east and south walls had to be torn down and rebuilt, and the interior required total rehabilitation. In January 1987 we opened the food pantry and the soup kitchen. The soup kitchen was well received, and by 1995 we averaged two hundred and fifty people per meal, three days each week.

As we had for many years, we continued to commemorate Martin Luther King's birthday in mid-January with an act of public witness. We held one memorable celebration in a vacant lot. Our friend Fr. Joe Muth, a Baltimore City parish priest and activist, celebrated a Eucharist, and we remembered Dr. King and all those who are forced to sleep in the open weather. Another year we constructed a three hundred and fifty pound Stone of Hope and planted it on our lot. On the stone we painted Dr. King's words, "Out of a mountain of despair we shall hew a stone of hope." It has been on the lot for three decades and is treated with utmost respect by all.

We will never forget the celebration of Dorothy Day's ninetieth birthday in 1987. The Los Angeles and Las Vegas Catholic Workers organized the event in Las Vegas. Cesar Chavez, founder of the United Farm Workers, Brazilian Archbishop of the poor Dom Helder Camara, and Catholic Workers from everywhere shared their visions for a just world. It ended, of course, with more than two hundred of us being arrested at the Nevada Test Site.

From 1995 to 2004, our daughter, Kate, and her husband, David Walsh-Little, whom she had married in 1995, lived and worked at Viva House. Their daughters Maya and Grace were born here, and Kate was pregnant with Julia during that time. In addition to helping with the soup kitchen, the Walsh-Littles infused new life and introduced new ideas into the work at the house.

After completing law school at Columbia University, Dave set up the Sowebo Center for Justice at Viva House. He practiced "backyard justice," setting up a simple card table in the backyard during the hours of the soup kitchen. He helped people with a wide range of legal problems from criminal charges to the loss of federal benefits. He also helped people understand their basic legal rights.

While living at Viva House, Dave also began representing death row inmate, John Booth-El. In addition to defending the poor and oppressed, Dave also supported protestors arrested for exercising their civil liberties.

I was in fact his first client in Maryland. I was arrested and charged for demonstrating at the Inner Harbor. The prosecution decided not to proceed to trial in the case. Additionally Dave helped other local activists, including the Gods of Metal plowshares, two priests, two nuns and one Catholic Worker, who were charged and tried in United States District Court for an action at Andrews Air Force Base.

While Dave ran the law office, Kate taught at the local elementary school to support their family's needs. During the summers, she organized Camp Sowebo for kids in the neighborhood who also attended her school. Many Viva House supporters shared their time and space with the camp. Fred and Bonnie Davis and Dave and Nancy Connell led some of the best swimming, boating, tubing, and water skiing tours around! Many other friends offered their pools, hiking trails, and donations for field trips. We were fortunate to have use of the St. Mary's Seminary van to transport the campers. The kids in our neighborhood enjoyed experiences they had never been exposed to.

In 1998, Kate and our friend Shannon Curran started a school year initiative called Full Circle: A Family Program at Viva House. This was primarily a tutoring program but also included many other ways of connecting with the children and their families. Volunteers tutored students ranging from second to fifth grade, with lessons that focused on improvement of specific skills. Theater and art were infused into the program as well as cooking, snacks, and field trips combined with Sr. Mary Ann Hartnett's after school program, Food for Thought.

These new ideas were more personal in approach, grounded in more of a one-to-one relationship. Quite a bit different from the enormous scale of the soup kitchen and food pantry. They helped us to remember to be neighbor, not agency. Having young children in the community accentuated the work and brought a new aspect to connecting with the neighborhood. With Maya, Grace, and Julia's help, Kate started the Viva House Play Group, which met once a week on the first floor of the house. The children and grandchildren of volunteers and neighbors gathered to build friendships and create a loving environment for the kids. In 2004, the Walsh-Littles moved from Viva House but continue to be a part of the work here. Kate still teaches children in impoverished Baltimore City public schools, and Dave continues to defend the rights of the poor by trying felony cases at Baltimore City's Office of the Public Defender.

We now know four generations of neighbors. They are old friends. We have watched each other's families grow up as we grow old. The unemployed and the underemployed come to our door with impossible bills for rent, utilities, water, medicine, and burials, and we do our best to help them. Given the state of Sowebo's economy, many neighbors will be debt ridden forever. Willa and I are both over seventy, and we are doing quite well. The community of saints in Baltimore has stood with us for almost a half century. Some bring food. Some bring money. Some bring blankets in the winter and fans in the summer. Committed workers have welcomed and served thousands of people and distributed tons of food bags all these years. It would be impossible for us to name all those who have supported the Catholic Worker here in Baltimore over the years. We don't want to slight anyone, but we note that among those working the soup kitchen these days are Mike Chovonec, Nancy and Dave Connell, Fred Davis, Rosemary Dew, Jack Garvey, Sr. Mary Ann Hartnett, Jean Krieger, Laura Lippman, Xavarian brothers John Mahoney, and Jerry O'Leary, Joan Muth, Peter Naughton, Carol Rosen, Beverly Schnetzler, Larry Ballentine, Joe Brady, Deborah Callard, Lauralee and Dick Humphrey, Eleanor Lewis, Sue Oppenheimer, Peggy Patti, Courtney Petersen, Andre Papantonio, Rod Ryon, Monique Shapiro, Nickie Sommerfeldt, Timothy Thompson, Tom Trager, SM., Mary and Lou Trianafilou, and Ann Watson. Our daughter Kate and our grandchildren Maya, Grace, and Julia have always helped out in the summer months, as do many other friends.

It has been quite a ride. And as long as our health holds up and as long as we can still lift the steaming pots, we will make it for a half century. Alleluia! Yes, indeed. Quite a ride.

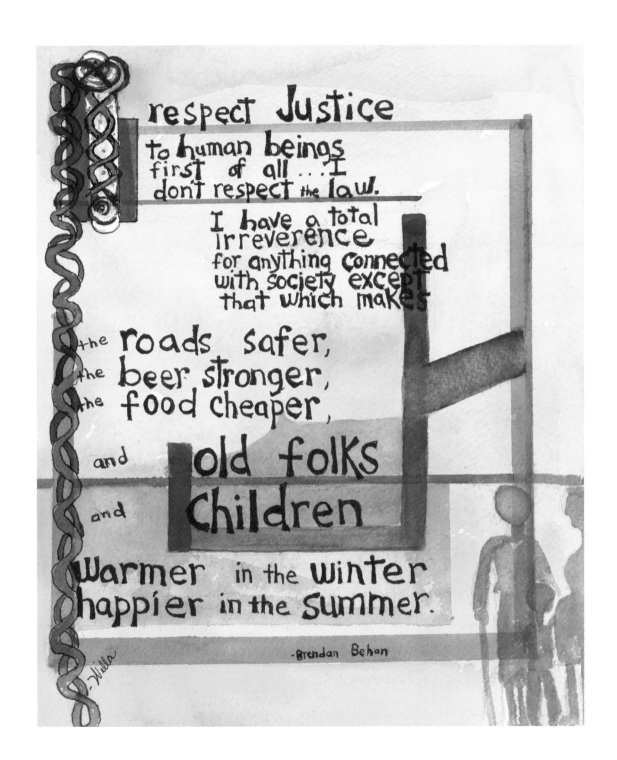

respect Justice to human beings first of all ...I don't respect the law.

I have a total irreverence for anything connected with society except that which makes

the roads safer, the beer stronger, the food cheaper, and old folks and children

warmer in the winter happier in the summer.

—Brendan Behan

15

All women of every land will WEAVE a world web to entangle the powers that bury our children.
~ from "Sing a Battle Song," poems by women in the Weather Underground

Chapter 2: Stories Along the Way

Stoopin', Strollin', and Swingin' • 2001

Nothing compares to being a grandparent. When you're with the very young, you move a little slower, you reflect a little deeper, and you tend to smile effortlessly and frequently. I think our granddaughter Maya is an outside kid. She's always been invigorated by the sounds, the smells, and the rhythm of the street. So, we've gone outside quite a bit during her first fifteen months. In Sowebo "outside" involves a lot of stoopin', strollin', and swingin'.

Stoopin.'

Stoopin' means you sit on the front steps of your house. The stoop is actually part of the sidewalk. It consists of four marble slabs and two handrails. For inner city folks, the stoop serves as your front porch and your front yard. It's a place to entertain, sip coffee, and come face to face with all the realities of the day. Some are glorious. Others tear you up.

I've been stoopin' for thirty-two years. Maya's working on her second. If nothing else, stoopin' keeps us alert. Cars, trucks, and buses stream by endlessly. And there are sirens 24/7. Fire trucks, ambulances (known around here as ambos), and police sirens pierce all five senses. Maya's already had a lifetime dosage of decibels.

The omnipresent PO-leese roll by too. They stare at us. We stare back. They are an occupying force in Sowebo.

Former Mayor Martin O'Malley referred to neighborhoods like ours as war zones. So, his PO-leese were busy establishing beachheads, securing corners, controlling the population. We don't encounter Officer Friendly down here. Usually, we're confronted with GI Joe.

The PO-leese are ever-vigilant, always on the prowl for addicts, pushers, prostitutes, the poor in general. Rarely are our neighbors seen as human beings created in the image of God. In my thirty-two years here, I've never seen the Po-leese searching for landlords who defraud their tenants by renting housing unfit for human habitation. In a war zone I guess some crimes, particularly the ones that violate justice, are permissible.

At our soup kitchen we share meals with all of our neighbors. So the lame, the jobless, and the blind break bread with the addicts, the prostitutes, and their children. If our neighborhood is a war zone and if many of our guests are considered the enemy, one could logically conclude that we give aid and comfort to the enemy.

In my early years of stoopin,' most people living in Sowebo seemed to be working. If you sipped a cup of morning coffee on the stoop, you could greet them on their way to a job. Some were headed to the Montgomery Ward warehouse and store a few blocks south of us. Others trekked to the light manufacturing plants surrounding nearby Carroll Park. Still others rode buses to places like Bethlehem Steel or to downtown offices and stores. People walked with a purpose. There was a job out there. Most of them were the working poor. Their wages just about paid the bills and kept families together. Or so it seemed.

Until the 1980s, lots of children lived and played on our block. The stoops were filled with children. Our daughter, Kate, never lacked playmates. Life was hard indeed, but people weren't so desperate as they are now. I wish Maya could have been stoopin' back then.

Now stoopin' teaches you more about despair than hope. You see it on the faces of people as they walk by. Our neighbors are either without work or are being paid woefully unjust wages without benefits. They do indeed explode the myth that the answer to poverty is always and simply a job. For the so-called unskilled and under-educated, the only jobs available do not pay a living wage. In fact, the Baltimore City Department of Social Services, with its workfare requirements, now works hand in hand with low-wage employers. Our tourist economy flourishes on the backs of the poor, who are paid minimum wages at best for service jobs.

In Baltimore, a select few live among grandiose symbols of prosperity and wealth—yachts, obscenely expensive ballparks, and the downtown Disneyland known as the Inner Harbor. But when you leave the harbor and travel into real neighborhoods, you encounter the poor, now formally renamed The Enemy. And we are at war with them. Each day in the U.S. we build one hundred new jail cells. Two million people are already locked up in our jails. What kind of a world are we giving Maya?

Strollin'

Strollin' with Maya is the opportunity of a lifetime. She's growing rapidly, and her days in a stroller are numbered. So as often as we can, we seize the time. Maya stretches out in her wee chariot and off we go. Her eyes miss nothing. The smallest scrap of paper blowing down the street fascinates her. Each tiny weed bursting through tired concrete catches her bright eyes. And she squeals with delight whenever she observes a bird, a dog, or best of all, other kids running and laughing.

When you stroll with a baby, everyone says "Hello!" It's the most humanizing of experiences. A real upper. Often we meet folks who come to the soup kitchen. It's a more personal meeting. At the soup kitchen there's a crowd, and it's too impersonal. So, Maya and I enjoy the spontaneity of meeting folks on the street one on one.

Strollin' in Sowebo has a downside, however. In block after block we meet massive destruction. It's as if someone in authority awakened from a drunken stupor, stumbled into Sowebo, and said, "Let's wreck the place and scatter the people." When students from the University of Michigan stayed with us, they were shocked. Was Baltimore involved in some unreported war? Who won? Why so many broken houses, so much rubble, so much garbage? We explained as best we could. Federal and local officials have agreed upon a scorched earth policy for all the inner cities of our country. So, we don't enforce housing code violations. We don't repair streets in poverty-stricken neighborhoods. We don't create parks or build recreation centers for all the youth in those neighborhoods. Pacification a la Vietnam! Then, government officials hope the poor will go elsewhere, anywhere. Who cares if they have to live in these uninhabitable conditions? And if anybody gets out of hand, then we have prison, the real housing for the poor.

Strollin' with Maya brings back memories. During Viva House's first year, 1968, our parish, St. Martin's, was home to a grade school, a high school, a convent for nuns, and a rectory with priests. Today there is no grade school, no high school, no convent, and no priests living in the rectory. And during the past two years, the church was closed completely. No more Sunday Mass. No more baptisms. No more weddings. I try to explain this to Maya. I think she gets the picture.

Strollin' down to the corner where Frederick Avenue meets Gilmor Street, I pause at the fence where police officer Darryl DeSousa killed Gerrett (Scooter) Jackson. I tell Maya that this is a holy place, and we have kept in contact with Scooter's mother for several years. Officer DeSousa, the man who murdered Scooter, is still out there battling the forces of evil and protecting property. So, a senseless killing, a grievous murder.

You can grow weary strollin' in Sowebo, and often Maya falls asleep. Time to go home.

Swingin'

Swingin' is another of Maya's favorite recreations. Since she was four months old, Maya had thoroughly enjoyed swingin' in those well-constructed, rubberized swings designed specifically for infants and toddlers. She literally soared toward the clouds and was delighted with the ride.

Locating a safe and well-equipped playground in Sowebo is a problem though. We have two choices. One is in the unit block of North Fulton Street. The other is on North Mount Street outside the Martin Luther King Center, highlighted in the book, *The Corner: A Year in the Life of an Inner-City Neighborhood* by David Simon and Edward Burns. Once we arrive at either of these sites, we encounter two difficulties. First, at any given time, at least half the swings are down. Second, trash, especially sharp pieces of glass, covers the area. So I carry Maya over the rubble and claim one of the working swings.

You begin to wonder. How come Sowebo's playgrounds are a mess? Viva House is directly across the street from Steuart Hill Academic Academy. Its play area is boring, broken asphalt. It does not re-create anyone. It does not inspire creativity. In truth, there is no playground.

One weekend morning I spotted a group of adults walking through the play area. They were scribbling notes on yellow pads. This is great, I thought. These folks are planning a new playground for the school. I went over to speak with them and was unpleasantly surprised. They told me they weren't planning a new playground. They were just taking notes on how *not* to build a playground. Ours was a perfect example.

We don't limit Maya's swingin' to Sowebo. We travel to various places in search of playgrounds that work. Federal Hill Park a couple of miles south of us is an excellent example. At this park, everything works. Swings, slides, a sandbox, and a large, grassy area undefiled by trash, broken glass, or dog feces make for one top-notch playground. The park also has a caretaker. In the Bronx we used to call them "the parkees." At any rate, the park is well kept up. Why, it even has a drinking fountain that works and a toilet, too.

The closest green space near Viva House is Union Square Park. Years ago, the city dumped one-quarter of a million dollars into renovating the park. Workers installed a delightful fountain. Now, the toilets are locked. The drinking fountain has been turned off. The fountain has become a place for trash.

Author Jonathan Kozol often writes about the "savage inequalities" that are so evident in all of our cities. If you pay more property taxes, you get better schools, better playgrounds, better services. If you merely use the services and if you are poor, you get spit in the face. You get repression. If you are a black male between the ages eighteen and thirty-two and you live in Baltimore's inner city, you get jail.

I make no effort to explain all of this to Maya. But if she keeps stoopin', strollin', and swingin' for a few more years, I know she'll begin to understand. She'll get the picture. She'll know globaloney when she sees it. She'll know all about "savage inequalities." And one day, when Maya is older and wiser, she might ask, "Grampa, how come the two hundred and twenty-five richest people in the world have a combined wealth of over one trillion dollars, equal to the combined annual income of the poorest 47 percent of the world's people?" I can only reply that once you allow small inequalities, the big inequalities become enormous. "Remember when you were very young, and you wanted to go to a park with swings that worked how we had to travel over to Federal Hill Park? That park had swings, water fountains, and fresh green grass, but there was nothing of equal beauty in our neighborhood." When Baltimore city residents allow seemingly small inequalities to flourish, they create a divided city, a lonely city, a city ripe for riots.

If You Live Alone • *2008*

Following in the footsteps of her big sister, Maya, our seven-year-old granddaughter Grace is reading now, and she is quite impressive. We were sitting in our living room a few days before Holy Week, and Grace read aloud the words on one of Willa's watercolor paintings.

She read the words with ease. "If you live alone, whose feet will you wash?" Immediately she asked what the words meant. A literal reading was a beginning. Understanding the deeper meaning of the words was a big second step. Acting on that deeper meaning could be an important goal.

Grace grasped the main point quickly. She knew she was part of a loving family and she did not live alone. She was also aware that we all had to do something if another person was in need. Grace had served meals at the soup kitchen many times, and the act of washing a person's feet made sense to her. After all, she has witnessed many of our neighbors asking for shoes or socks and a measure of comfort for feet that were tired and often severely damaged. I told her about the foot clinic at Atlanta's Open Door Community. They consider the washing of feet to be a sacrament. It certainly trumps Confirmation and is perhaps on the same level as the Eucharist and Baptism.

In this country we make great efforts to "live alone," to isolate ourselves from our neighbors. And you don't see many people washing another's feet. Community is not a major concern. We don't stress the common good or that we need one another. We're rugged individualists. Making money, getting a leg up on our neighbor—that's our value system. In our neighborhoods and in our relations with the rest of humankind, we settle disputes with absolute violence.

A few days after my conversation with Grace, I was walking to Bon Secours Hospital. While waiting for the light to change at the corner of Baltimore and Monroe streets, I was approached by a child. He was no older than Grace. He asked me what I wanted today. Then I realized that I was standing on the corner of the day's open air drug market, and the youngster was merely working the block. Across the street, two teenagers were running the show. I told him I was good for the day and crossed the street.

This wasn't an isolated incident. The child was younger than others I had seen working the drug trade. Sadly, the drug business employs many of the people in our neighborhood. It is the backbone of Sowebo's economy. But we must worry about the child's welfare. Was he trying to get some money for himself, for his family? Was he living alone? Did anyone ever listen to him read aloud? What will happen to him today? Tomorrow? Next week?

And what does this say about the neighborhood where he is trying to become a man?

Standing Up for the Worm • 2015

It was a halcyon day in Sowebo. The weather was clear, cool, and refreshing. All of our windows were opened wide, and I was dozing.

The tranquility was broken by the cheerful voice of our nine-year-old neighbor. He was squealing, "Look, I found a worm! Look! A worm!" He was elated with his discovery, and he rushed to show it to his sister and brother. Oh, was he fascinated!

His mother was inside their house and came to the back door. The giggling of the children woke her from an afternoon nap. Her only thought was, "You don't want that freakin' worm. Kill the freakin' thing! It's just a dirty, slimy piece of crap. Kill the freakin' worm!"

The boy was puzzled. He said, "But, Mama, it's living. It's cute and small and isn't bothering anyone." His mother was annoyed now and wouldn't stand for any back talk. "I told you to kill the freakin' worm. Now!" The boy, sobbing, did as he was told.

I walked away from the window and went out our front door. I thought about my granddaughter Julia, who had just become a vegan. She would have stood up for the rights of all living things. She would have stood up for the worm.

I should have stood up for the worm. I should have stood with the boy.

Clinging to Love • 2008

He pointed the gun in my face a few minutes before 5 a.m. The gun was similar to those carried by the police. He was maybe fifteen or sixteen years old, and he mumbled, "This is for real" or something similar.

I had just started my daily two-mile exercise walk around Union Square Park. When you walk at 5 a.m., you escape the heat and the dangerous rays of the sun.

When the young man stopped me, I was directly across the street from the front door of Steuart Hill Academic Academy, the school Kate once attended. The young man was riding on the back of a bicycle, and his friend was doing the pedaling.

They approached me from the rear. The surprise was overwhelming, and my fear is impossible to explain. With the gun staring me in the face, I thought this was my last walk. This was the way my forty years of living and working in Southwest Baltimore were going to end. I was wearing old, grey gym shorts, well-worn running shoes, and a T-shirt bearing the words "Grampa Rocks," a gift from my three granddaughters.

Immediately, I turned the pockets of my shorts inside out, showing the youngster I had no money and carried only a house key. I purposely did not make eye contact, did not raise my voice, and tried not to panic. My daughter tells her three daughters to "use their words, not their hands" when faced with conflict. I explained to the young man that I was just getting exercise.

And, then, he let me go. "Just go home then," he muttered. He walked back to the bike, and the two boys disappeared down South Gilmor Street.

So there you have it. In the morning darkness, a teenager telling a sixty-five-year-old grandpa to "just go home."

I walked to West Lombard Street and noticed a couple getting into their car. I explained to them what had just happened, urged them to be careful, and requested a ride to Viva House, only a block away.

I don't know why he let me go—why I wasn't killed or badly beaten. Was it the words on my shirt? Did he recognize me from Viva House? Maybe he or some relative or friend had shared a meal at our soup kitchen or carried home groceries from our pantry. I'll never know.

Over the last forty years, thousands of Baltimoreans have been murdered. Even more have experienced terrible violence. I thought it was my turn.

To celebrate Viva House's fortieth anniversary in October 2008, we hung a banner on the front of our house. It reads simply: "Love One Another." I am not giving up on that idea.

The Apology • 2010

It was one of those Tuesdays. I was on the phone. Above our roof a police helicopter buzzed and raged over and over again. Then I heard the sound of police cars screeching to a halt in the alley on the side of our house. At the same moment someone was pushing the front door bell repeatedly.

I hung up the phone immediately and rushed to the back yard. The police were just checking one of the many abandoned houses. Much sound. More fury. They found nothing. Saw no one. They left.

Then I remembered the front door. I opened it and found blood everywhere. Blood on the door. Blood on every step. A bloody trail on the sidewalk. I saw no one down or up the street. Was there a connection between the police in the alley and the blood out front? Puzzled, I washed off the blood.

The next day, during the soup kitchen, a young man stopped me as I was working and apologized for bleeding on the front steps. He told me he had come to the house for some canned goods, but after he rang the doorbell, three men jumped him, bloodied his head, and left him on the ground. Then, they apologized to him. They thought he was someone else.

I gave him the last of the canned goods. He apologized once again for bleeding on the steps. What would have happened if he had been the man they were looking for? Life in Sowebo.

Lamentations of Baltimore

O Baltimore,
how lonely you sit.
Once you were thronged
with nearly a million people.
Now it's as if
you were suddenly widowed.
You've prostituted yourself
to the developers, the privileged,
the silver-spooned people.
You permit families
to be dumped on the cold
streets while you hurry by
to your yachts and ball games. COME, God of liberation!
Two thousand years on . . .
We don't need much—
some bread, a place to rest,
and plenty, plenty of roses.
We, the poor,
are forgotten—
As good as dead
in your heart
Something to be discarded,
people not to be tolerated.
COME, O God of the oppressed! Don't let Baltimore
shame and dishonor us.
Don't let her
discredit us and build bank accounts on our weary backs.

—Inspired by the book of Lamentations and Psalm 25

Snapshots of Sowebo

The only kinds of fights worth having are those that you're going to lose, because somebody has to fight them and lose and lose and lose until someday, somebody who believes as you do wins. In order for somebody to win an important, major fight 100 years hence, a lot of other people have to be willing—for the sheer fun and joy of it—to go right ahead and fight, knowing you're going to lose. You mustn't feel like a martyr. You've got to enjoy it.
—*I.F. Stone*

Forty years on and for us there is no turning back. We agree with Izzy Stone that indeed there is joy in the struggle. Yes, we have lost most of the battles, but there is a measure of truthfulness when you try to give a human face to those who suffer. There is hope when you actually name the evil and do your best to confront it.

We've confronted unemployment, homelessness, hunger, inadequate health care, the sheer lunacy of Baltimore's drug war, the death penalty, torture, all the dirty wars from Vietnam to Iraq, and the eternal war the rich have been waging on the poor. And victories have been elusive. There have been individual success stories, but as we have learned too well, there are no individual solutions to deep-rooted, systemic problems.

Dorothy Day told us that all we can do is plant the seeds of hope and perhaps another generation will reap a harvest of justice.

What follows are some remembrances and a glimpse into what we have seen and done and heard. Glorious years. Hard times. Learning and yearning. Bread and wine. Hunger and thirst. Dreams and nightmares.

Ode to a Daffodil

In the early 1980s a woman named Lois lived with us. She was one of the gentlest women we have ever met. And she wrote gentle poetry. On Holy Saturday 1983, she went downtown and admired the hundreds of daffodils planted in front of an office building on Pratt Street. She thought the flowers would be perfect for Easter and proceeded to pick at least one hundred blooms. She appeared to be official and no one questioned her. So, at Viva House we celebrated the Resurrection with bright yellow daffodils. Not long after that Lois slipped a few poems through our mail slot and traveled to another city.

A Good Compliment

I can live for two months on a good compliment.
—Mark Twain

After finishing his meal one glorious winter day, a young man paused at the back gate and said, "You know what I like about this soup kitchen?"

Two of us were on our way into the house, but we stopped to hear his comment. We were thinking that he really enjoyed a superb meal, or was moved by the rich art work hanging on our walls, or most importantly, was delighted by the friendly workers who were serving that day. "The thing I like," he said, "is that when you leave here, you don't have to go back to your cell." A real Sowebo compliment.

Locked In, Locked Out

During one of Baltimore's brutally hot summer days, a nine-year-old boy came to our door requesting a drink of water. I gave him several glasses and he gulped them down. Knowing he lived just down the street, I asked why he didn't go home to get out of the heat. He said that his mom went to work early in the morning, and whenever she leaves, she locks the house tight. So the boy had a choice to stay in or out of the house. Either way, the house would be locked to keep out robbers. So a nine year old wanders the streets all day. No public toilets. No drinking fountains.

The Pianist

The happiness of your life depends upon the quality of your thoughts.
—Marcus Aurelius

One day in early spring a man stopped by the house. We know him as John, and he said earnestly, "I need to play the piano for a few minutes." We're accustomed to the usual request for food, clothing, money, water, the phone, or help filling out some government form. But not that day. The request was to play the piano.

We invited him in, got him settled, and went back upstairs. He played and played and played. And he belted out some powerful gospel tunes. John had come to announce the good news. His concert was breathtaking. He was soaring with the eagles. For a precious few moments he escaped all the decay of Baltimore, and he took us with him.

At the end of an hour and a half, he drank several glasses of iced tea and left. John really needed to play the piano. I'll remember that when they blow up the next public housing units, making even more people homeless. People need bread. People need music too. Life in Sowebo.

He Lived in One Room

God has always been hard on the poor.
—Jean Paul Marat

During the summer of 2001, we delivered a brand new bed to an elderly neighbor in need of the barest essentials. He lived in one room. The room was on the first floor of an apartment building in the unit block of South Fulton Street, one of the fiercest blocks in Baltimore. Our neighbor paid a whopping $250 a month in rent for the privilege of living in a closet. The room had no toilet, no kitchen. Just four walls, a door, and two windows. For security our neighbor had nailed his windows shut, and for added protection, he nailed boards in front of them. When we delivered the bed the outside temperature was ninety-two degrees. Imagine how hot it was in the room.

Water

You know, peoples was not meant to be dogged around. Peoples was made to be respected.
—Jerome Bowden, Open Door Community, Atlanta, Georgia

On August 17, 2002, the afternoon heat was fierce. We were walking to the corner of Mount and Lombard streets when we saw a man crouched on the sidewalk. He was slurping water from a white plastic bowl that had been placed in the shade of an anemic tree. An elderly neighbor regularly filled this bowl with water for stray cats and dogs. But this day a full grown man beat them to it. We helped him to his feet and offered him a cold soda. A small comfort. Free drinking water is hard to find, and public restrooms are becoming a memory. So a man is reduced to this.

31

Chapter 3: Saints Keep Appearing

Saints are human beings we celebrate for their uniqueness, for their gifts—good and bad—and for their ability to help us understand both suffering and joy.

An Expensive Death • 1976

Kenny was one of the first people we got to know in Sowebo. He was one of our first teachers about life and death on Baltimore streets.

Kenny was a small, graceful, intelligent, and unhappy man. He was born and raised in Baltimore's inner city. He was poor and alcoholic. He needed to be saved.

Kenny's life was excruciatingly painful. He drank but usually did not eat. He rested but never felt secure enough to sleep. Young kids, taking advantage of his defenselessness, often stoned him for sport or robbed and beat him in broad daylight. Part of Kenny's neighborhood was experiencing "historic preservation," and quite often Kenny would be arrested for dozing on a park bench. When responding to the charge of vagrancy, Kenny would often be found in contempt of court. He would protest rather loudly that he could not understand how city authorities could always provide twelve feet of space for cars to park but not one foot of space for a human being to sleep. Long time Chicago Catholic Worker Karl Meyer made this same observation years before. No matter. This bit of logic usually cost Kenny dearly—a few more days in the city jail.

Kenny was a worn-out veteran of every alcoholism treatment program in the city, and when he was really desperate, he would find a way to gain admission to a hospital. He did this whenever he felt confronted by death. The hospital had clean sheets, warmth, hot food, a well-intentioned staff, and relative security. It provided competent primary nursing care and a therapeutic community. The hospital tried to save Kenny, and while he was hospitalized, it always appeared that rehabilitation and reform were near at hand. He was always referred to as a model patient.

But, alas, hospitalization terminated after thirty days (that was a long time ago—now you are treated as an outpatient). Kenny would be back on the streets.

One day three weeks after his forty-first birthday, four days after his most recent hospitalization, and midway between the frenzy of Thanksgiving and Christmas, Kenny was found bloodied and dead on the second floor of an abandoned house. This house was in the shadow of a newly renovated, historically preserved masterpiece. Kenny had been dead more than a week. Freezing weather and gnawing rats left their horrible marks.

One of his friends, a man who had shared many pints with Kenny, told the police that Kenny really wanted to stop drinking, but there was no reason for him to want to be conscious in our society. He could neither read nor write. There were no jobs for him. He often muttered to himself that he wanted to live, but the system was dead.

Kenny died for no reason. That is why his death cost so much. Even more expensive than the enormous military budget planned for the new year.

¡Kenny, presente!

After All is Said and Done • 1982

Betty lived with us on and off for about three years. She was pleasant and kept to herself. After all was said and done, she never got permanent housing.

Betty was a frail, grey-haired woman who carried a black purse everywhere. She had a most delightful smile and a unique style. It is a matter of public record that she was never involved in the research, development, or deployment of nuclear weapons. She was a gentle woman who was well known for one expression, "after all is said and done." This expression was usually followed by "I was robbed" or "I lost my place" or "they don't do anything to help you anyway."

Betty bothered no one. In turn she was bothered by seizures and homelessness.

One day she found herself in Baltimore. She was told that the city was in the midst of a renaissance, but she wondered about this strange rebirth. The people she encountered daily weren't being born, they were dying. The people Betty knew were in deep trouble. Some were without jobs. Many had psychiatric afflictions. All of them were destitute and searching.

Betty didn't know about the renaissance. She was more familiar with the suffering.

Life in Baltimore was a constant struggle. Repeatedly, she was robbed of her Social Security checks. In the colder months she traveled from temporary shelter to temporary shelter. She mistrusted social workers and often mused that they too robbed her, not by force but by indifference. Betty longed for the warm weather months, a time of independence, a time when there was no need for temporary shelters and no time for social workers, a time when she could make it on her own.

Betty enjoyed spending hours at the city's harbor. It was a warm and, she thought, somewhat safe place. She had chosen her particular space for resting day and night. And she could often be found in a mall called Harborplace.

Harborplace, the golden calf of Baltimore's pitch for tourism dollars, was fast becoming a regular hangout for the homeless. Folks were beginning to stake out semipermanent residences there. Those without the necessities of life could sit and watch those with the necessities buy things that were not necessary. Harborplace management didn't like what it saw. They summoned security officers to herd the homeless out.

On a cool evening in mid-June, Betty was ushered out of Harborplace. With black purse in hand she walked to the docking area of the Port Welcome, a sightseeing boat. She sat down next to the boat and disappeared.

To this day no one is exactly sure what happened. But somehow Betty slipped into the harbor and was dragged under the Port Welcome. Her black purse lay on the dock and was discovered by a security officer in the morning.

A few days later, after the Port Welcome pulled out of port, Betty's body floated to the surface. Her death was duly reported as "death by drowning."

At her burial service a handful of people said that Betty may have been found dead in the water, but it was homelessness that killed her. After all is said and done, Betty was not welcome in Baltimore, or at least not at the place where the golden calf was built. *¡Betty, presente!*

Double Dose of Peace and Healing • 1986

In whatsoever houses I enter, I will enter to help the sick, and I will abstain from all wrongdoing and harm, especially from abusing the bodies of man or woman, bond or free.
—*Hippocrates,* The Physician's Oath

Lee Randol was a doctor everyone should have known. He made house calls and was able to diagnose both individual illnesses and the systemic diseases of violence and greed that are devouring this nation.

The death of Dr. C. Lee Randol is a loss not just to the Baltimore community but to the world community as well. These days, people of peace and healing are rare indeed.

Viva House knew Lee for almost twenty years. He struggled with us and went to jail with us. He cared for us when we were sick and gave us hope when we were weary.

Lee's gentle compassion brought him into many homes. Countless children in the Baltimore area grew strong with Lee as their physician. He made house calls, and they were unique. Whenever our daughter, Kate, was ill, Lee would come to the house, make his diagnosis, write a prescription, and then excuse himself for a few minutes. He would go to the local pharmacy and fill the prescription at his expense. If he thought the illness would make us parents anxious, often he would bring back a bottle of wine to calm our anxiety.

Lee understood that a diagnosis without a prescription was meaningless. When he found something was wrong, he went into action. We were to learn that this principle guided his life.

As a pediatrician, he had a keen understanding of the slaughter taking place in Vietnam. He knew that it was indeed a land of burning children, and he joined the antiwar movement early. He wrote to Congress and letters to the editor. He walked picket lines and joined mass marches on Washington.

In the summer of 1973, for no logical, legal, or humane reason, this country unleashed tons of bombs on Cambodia for six solid weeks. Small groups of people began a month-long experiment in nonviolent, direct action at the White House. Four or five people would join a White House tour and then step away from the tourists to pray publicly that the bombings would cease until they were arrested.

Lee, antiwar activists Tom Ireland and Jim LaCroce, and I were part of the second pray-in. During the arrest procedure, Lee refused to cooperate and would not give basic information about himself. As a result, the four of us spent a long weekend in underground Washington waiting for arraignment.

Lee, the doctor, was a dilemma for the courts. He was teaching the Department of Justice that the carpet bombing of children was bad medicine. He was teaching all of us the physician's oath, *Primum non nocere* (First, do no harm).

Our admiration for the man grew over two decades. Lee was the first doctor to step forth unflinchingly to launch the Baltimore People's Free Medical Clinic (currently the People's Community Health Center). He understood that the Vietnam War was a foreshadowing of future conflict in Central America. Thus, right up to his death, he worked tirelessly with the Baltimore Sanctuary Movement and Amnesty International. In a real way, the children in El Salvador and Nicaragua were healed by Lee's involvement.

During his memorial service at Stony Run Friends Meeting House in Baltimore, friends shared vivid recollections of Lee Randol. Someone noted that he was a shy and mysterious person who avoided personal recognition. Another prayed for a double dose of Lee's spirit so we could confront the nuclear violence all around us.

Yes, Lee believed that only life was the healer of life. He brought the love of life into all the houses he entered. *¡Lee Randol, presente!*

In Sowebo Angels Come and Go • 1995

I heard the gunshots that killed Gerrett Tyrone "Scooter" Jackson. He was shot in the head, and there was no inquiry. We protested at police headquarters, but there were no uprisings then, like those occurring later in Ferguson, Missouri, or Baltimore, when Freddie Gray died in police custody. No one had video cameras in 1995 like they do now.

In 1995 Mount Street is being invaded. The police are here big time. They come on bikes. They ride motorcycles. They drive cars, marked and unmarked. They wear uniforms, and they dress in civilian clothes. They harass everyone. And they make numerous arrests.

You have to do a reality check. Is this Chiapas? Or East Timor? Or the North of Ireland? Men and women, mostly young, sometimes as many as twenty in number, are forced up against brick walls. Often they are ordered to lie face down on the cold concrete or to drop their pants while they are searched. Many are loaded into the ever-present wagons.

"Probable cause," they say.

"Looking for drugs," they say.

"We're here to help," they say.

Death is an inevitable consequence of the daily harassment.

Intimidation and harassment always lead to violence. So, on Friday, February 24, 1995, just before two o'clock in the afternoon, thirty-year-old mounted police officer Darryl DeSousa shot at twenty-six-year-old Gerrett Tyrone Jackson, "Scooter." He fired thirteen shots; the rapid fire could be heard for blocks. Ten bullets filled Mr. Jackson's young body. The police story differs from the people's witnesses. Officer DeSousa claims Mr. Jackson threatened him with a gun. It is clear that Mr. Jackson never fired a shot. Witnesses say that Mr. Jackson did not draw a weapon and was shot like a dog.

Here in Baltimore we have fire power. We have punishment. Now it appears police shoot to kill.

Now a man is dead. The harassment continues. Drugs still flow, if not on this corner then on another. Death is still in charge here.

We held a prayer service at the site of Scooter's murder. Only a few people attended. The police watched us closely. While we were praying, a young woman appeared. She sang Psalm 23: "My Shepherd is the Lord. . . . Fresh and green are the pastures where he gives me repose."

I have never heard this psalm sung or recited with more reverence.

When she finished the psalm, the woman left without a word. In Sowebo, angels come and go. *¡Scooter, presente!*

For Teresa and for All the Mothers in all the Calcuttas of this Earth • 1997

When we learned of Mother Teresa's funeral service, we compared it to the service for Dorothy Day. At Dorothy's funeral Mass, there were no military, no Catholic bishops, no police escort to the cemetery. Mostly common folk attended, and many of them were given parking tickets for double parking in front of the church.

I wish, Teresa,
there was
no state funeral, no military presence, no head of state, no power, no suits and ties.
But,
Let the mourners be just the ordinary folks,
what some call
the scum of God's earth,
Calcutta's driftwood, Baltimore's crack addict, those left to fester in their sores,
isolated criminalized
bereft of human dignity.
Let their voices shout in heavenly choir
WHY? WHY? WHY?
Teresa,
there are so many poor people
demanding so much mercy and justice,
that they overwhelm you and us.
You thought the powerful could provide assistance and answers.
You let them embrace you
in Haiti, in your own Albania, in the USA.
And for this embrace
you got their pocket change.
You helped to make them look good.
A grievous mistake.
A systemic mistake.
You thought those who pounded people into hell's ditch

actually cared about the people.
They were only concerned about the cost of the ditch.
And, so, Teresa, we gather to pray for you
and for all the mothers in all the Calcuttas of this earth.
Don't let them buy you off with sainthood.
Don't let them make you an irrelevant statue.
Instead, stand with Dorothy Day
and Oscar Romero and Malcolm X
and all the WHYS of this earth.
RISE FROM THE GRAVE!
TURN POWER, CHURCH AND STATE ON ITS HEAD!
And, when donations cease,
Pray Mary's Magnificat . . .
He has put down the mighty from their thrones.
He has exalted the lowly
and all those who ask
WHY? WHY? WHY?

Eulogy for Philip Francis Berrigan St. Peter Claver Church, Baltimore, Maryland December 9, 2002

Phil was a friend and brother in the struggle since 1967, and it was a great privilege to offer one of the eulogies at his funeral.

Philip Berrigan is our friend. And he is a friend to everyone gathered here today.

Philip Berrigan and his Jonah House community are friends of Dorothy Day, our Viva House community, and all the Catholic Worker houses throughout the world.

Philip Berrigan is a friend to all the poor in Baltimore City. You saw how we treat the poor when we walked over to the church this morning.

Philip Berrigan is a friend to all the people of the world who are bombed and scattered, who are starved, trampled upon, imprisoned, tortured, humiliated, scoffed at, dismissed as nobodies.

Philip Berrigan is a friend to all those people who are robbed and beaten and left for dead in ditches all over this planet.

Philip Berrigan knew, as Chief Sitting Bull said, that our insatiable "love of possessions was indeed a disease."

Phil was street savvy. He knew the streets around St. Peter Claver Church. And he understood the racism that still festers and still divides us as a nation. After the publication of Phil's first book, *No More Strangers*, in 1965, Stokely Carmichael observed that Phil Berrigan was one of the few white people in the United States who actually knew what was really going on.

Philip Berrigan knew the truth. He was a witness to the truth.

He was that rare person in whom word and deed were one. Always. Everywhere. Steadfast. Rock solid. Hopeful. One in a million. He was that tree standing by the water that would not be moved.

The Gospel was Phil's truth. He understood the meaning of the Mystical Body better than anyone we know. All of us are sisters and brothers to one another. And when one of us suffers an injury, all of us suffer an injury. It was that simple for Phil Berrigan. So, when the filthy rotten system that Dorothy Day wrote about threatens to tear us apart from one another, that system has to be resisted. Always. Everywhere.

Throughout his entire life—whether he was locked tight in the maximum security of our stinking jails or (as he would say with a wise old grin) living in the minimum security prison of Baltimore City— he fought, nonviolently, both the famine and the crown (as we Irish folks say). And he paid for it.

We had the privilege of knowing Phil for thirty-five of his seventy-nine years. And he was in prison for eleven of them. Think about it. That's almost one of every three days. And he never complained, never whined. No self-pity. If you received a letter from Phil in jail, you would never learn of the suffering he was enduring. During his last imprisonment, Phil must have struggled with intense pain in his hip. And surely the terrible cancer was assaulting his body. But, he never complained. He never complained! Indeed, Phil is a brother to the suffering servant described so magnificently by the prophet Isaiah.

And, as soon as he completed one stint in jail, he was organizing yet another nonviolent direct action. He always asked us to join him. He asks all of us to join him. Phil Berrigan would repeat for us today the last words of Joe Hill: "Don't mourn for me! Organize! Organize a general strike against the warmakers!"

And, why was Phil in jail all those years? Again, his simple answer: "We can't burn the planet down! We can't! And we won't let them burn the planet down. That's our Number 1 business." In 1967 and 1968, Phil told Presidents Johnson and Nixon that they can't burn our sisters and brothers in Vietnam with our napalm, our white phosphorous, our cluster bombs. With his last breath he told Bush, Chaney, Rumsfeld, and Ashcroft (you know the gang) that we won't let them bomb the people of Iraq and leave our depleted uranium, our nuclear garbage, scattered all over their land for decades to come. And we dare to call the Iraqis terrorists as we look down our guns, as we kill their children with our sanctions. And we dare to search for their weapons of mass destruction, while we, the mass murderers in Hiroshima, in Nagasaki, in Chile, in El Salvador, in Nicaragua, in Afghanistan, and in countless other places continue to design and build even more hideous weapons of mass destruction. Phil said it correctly, "We're the terrorists!"

Philp Berrigan was one intense brother. On May 17, 1968, the day of the Catonsville Draft Board raid, three people were designated to drive the nine resisters to the site. We gathered at the home of Al and Pauline Lewis, Tom Lewis's parents. I was to drive one of the cars. It was a St. Peter Claver parish car. Phil and Dan Berrigan would be passengers. When it was time to proceed to Catonsville, Phil grabbed the keys from me. He would do the driving. He would make sure the car would get there. He would make sure those draft files, those killing licenses, would be burned. As Dan Berrigan would write later, "It is better to burn paper than to napalm children." I will never forget the intensity. I thought about Jesus overturning the tables in the temple. Intensity.

Philip Berrigan was one honest brother, but we all know that. Even our kangaroo courts knew that. He scared them to death. I remember one trial. It was in the late seventies, I think. (Phil was on trial so many times that sometimes it's hard to remember when one began and one ended.) This trial involved pouring blood and ashes inside the Pentagon. I threw ashes. Phil threw blood. On the day of trial, the cop who arrested me failed to appear, so I walked. The cop who arrested Phil did show up and testified that Phil threw ashes. When Phil was asked what he did at the Pentagon, he simply stated that he threw blood. The judge, a difficult man who sentenced people harshly, dismissed the charges against Phil because of the cop's false testimony. He said, "In all the years that Mr. Berrigan has come before me, he never lied." I was elated, but Phil wasn't too happy about walking away.

On Dorothy Day's gravestone there are but two words: DEO GRATIAS. Thanks be to God!

Yes, Phil, Deo Gratias! Thanks be to God! For your life. For your spirit that is still with us. Now, with you gone to another place, all of us will have to do more. Phil often said, "Couragio!" Couragio to you, Phil! Now we say peace to you and us. *¡Phil Berrigan, presente!*

Another Sowebo Murder • 2005

It was hard to believe that Sam "Scooby" Umstead could be gunned down in the middle of the afternoon. To this day we know of no serious investigation into this murder.

On June 27, 2005, Viva House welcomed Ian Cunniffe and Danny Moore, our nephews from the Chicago area. Ian and Danny had come to work with us for a week, a tradition established with the Cunniffe and Moore clans for the last two decades.

In the afternoon, while we were orienting Ian and Danny to the house, we heard popping sounds in the alley on the north side of the house. We presumed they were firecrackers. In Sowebo, July Fourth begins on June first. So, a month of disturbing noise.

But this day was different. Just before four p.m., an ambulance rushed up the alley. I went out the front door, making no connection between the presumed firecracker noise and the ambulance. Willa joined me in the alley. A man was lying there, and two paramedics were trying to find a pulse. Willa identified herself as a nurse and asked if she could be of assistance. They asked her to bring the oxygen tank. But Sam, Scooby, was lying in a pool of blood. He had been shot in the head. There was no pulse.

Another Baltimore homicide. Another Sowebo murder. The third murder on our block since we opened Viva House. The police arrived, "full of sound and fury, signifying nothing." At one point, I counted twenty-seven cops, about half suit-and-tie detectives. They assured us the investigation was now underway. Unfortunately, we knew differently. The truth is no cop is looking for anyone connected to this murder. Scooby's death has been dismissed as just another drug-related homicide.

On Wednesday, June 29, while Scooby's blood still clung to the unforgiving pavement, we held a memorial service. Brother John Mahoney, CFX, one of our Wednesday workers, offered a prayer and a reflection. John said, "We don't know whether Scooby knew God, but we are sure that God knew Scooby, just as God knows all of us."

Ian and Danny had been in Baltimore for only a few hours and were shocked by this senseless killing. They asked many questions and volunteered to put together some music on a tape deck for the service. We covered Scooby's blood with flowers.

On the very next day, we met Scooby's son and his brother in the alley. They saw the flowers. They were overwhelmed with sorrow but were consoled that someone was with Scooby when he died.

A permanent wooden plaque now stands on our side yard in Scooby's memory. "In memory of Sam. May he now have the peace he never found on these streets. Rock of Hope." *¡Scooby, presente!*

Our Favorite Teacher • 2010

When I became a teacher, I could not possibly keep out of the classroom my own experiences. I have often wondered how so many teachers manage to spend a year with a group of students and never reveal who they are, what kind of lives they have led, where their ideas come from, what they believe in, or what they want for themselves, for their students, and for the world. In my teaching I never concealed my political views: my detestation of war and militarism, my anger at racial inequality, my belief in democratic socialism, in a rational and just distribution of wealth. The mixing of activism and teaching, this insistence that education can't be neutral in the crucial issues of our time, this movement back and forth from the classroom to the struggles outside by teachers who hope their students will do the same, has always frightened the guardians of traditional education. They prefer that education simply prepare the new generation to take its place in the old order, not to question that order.
—Howard Zinn, You Can't Be Neutral on a Moving Train

Author and political activist Naomi Klein was right. The passing of Howard Zinn means that "we have lost our favorite teacher." We have lost another great activist who stood shoulder to shoulder with the poor, the unemployed, the marginalized, the homeless, and with all those sisters and brothers who have suffered the terrible consequences of U.S. greed and militarism.

Howard presented history from the bottom up. He was not just another disinterested scholar, and he examined the past from the perspective of daily life as most of the world's people encounter it. His books, his speeches, his teaching were not deadening accounts of the victories of marauding generals or of the greedy deeds of rich white men.

I first met Howard Zinn in 1968. As an expert witness in the trial of the Baltimore Four, he had come to testify that pouring blood on 1A draft files was a truthful condemnation of the Vietnam War. Dave Eberhardt, Tom Lewis, Jim Mengel, and Phil Berrigan were trying to help our country out of an impossible quagmire. When they poured blood on draft files at a Baltimore Selective Service office in October 1967, only a few thousand U.S. troops had been killed. By the war's end, the total would exceed fifty-eight thousand. Needless to say, Baltimore's kangaroo court didn't permit Howard's testimony. As I recall, the court would not listen to any testimony that challenged the war.

I told Howard that Phil Berrigan had given me a copy of his book, *The Logic of Withdrawal*, when I first arrived in Baltimore. It was the first book I had read about Vietnam. I have read all of Howard's books since.

In the late 90s, Howard stayed with us at Viva House after delivering an inspiring lecture at the University of Maryland Baltimore County. It was a real treat for us, like spending a joyous evening with an old friend. We had only met twice, yet it seemed as if our conversation simply picked up where we had left off. I believe all of his students had a similar experience.

In November 2010, the folks at the Creative Alliance, an arts organization in Baltimore, presented a performance based on *Voices from a People's History of the United States*, a collection of primary sources that give voice to popular struggles compiled by Zinn and Anthony Arnove. Many cities have also done this. In Baltimore, seventeen people gave readings ranging from Bartolome De Las Casas's sixteenth century denunciation of Spanish colonial policy towards native peoples to Cindy Sheehan's twenty-first century protest of the Iraq War. It was marvelous. The house was packed for two performances. I had the honor of being Howard Zinn's voice and delivered excerpts of his November 1970 lecture at Johns Hopkins University. I had actually been in the audience for that talk; it was about the necessity of civil disobedience when dealing with forces that deprive people of life, liberty, and the pursuit of happiness. It was relevant in 1970. It is even more relevant now.

Howard Zinn. A truthful man. Principled. Wise. Gentle. Our favorite teacher. *¡Howard Zinn, presente!*

Alley of Tears • 2014

We are not expecting utopia here on earth. But God meant things to be much easier than we have made them.
—Dorothy Day

Oscar Torres was murdered on Memorial Day 2014. He lived down the street from Viva House, and we came to know his family in the days following his murder. We prayed with his family each evening before the day of his funeral, and we helped raise funds to return Oscar's body to Mexico for burial.

Sometimes you just get weary doing this work. You get tested all the time. And it is easy to get discouraged. It's possible to lose the joy and enthusiasm that is required to keep providing hospitality and doing resistance work.

We have been tested. We were growing weary. So we paused. We reexamined. We prayed. And we gathered our community, our co-workers and tried to comprehend Oscar's murder and the violence so common in Baltimore. We experienced some rough days. The senseless murder of Oscar Torres, the sting of his death, indeed the overwhelming poverty and violence that defines Baltimore's inner city neighborhoods, had a profound effect on us. It truly brought us to our knees.

On Memorial Day 2014 at 1 a.m., Oscar Torres, a fifteen-year-old young man, was shot in the head point blank. He died no more than twenty feet from our front door. He bled out adjacent to the Stone of Hope we had placed in our yard some years earlier. It is a bitter irony as we go searching for "hope on this side of the grave," to quote Irish poet Seamus Heaney. And to add to this bitterness, our three granddaughters, Maya, Grace, and Julia, were staying with us that night. Maya, the oldest, was also fifteen years old. The same age as Oscar.

Oscar lived on Mount Street, four blocks south of Viva House. His family is from Mexico. Oscar's parents, Francisco and Ernestine, and his brother, Julio, were overwhelmed with grief at Oscar's death. They could not be consoled. Some neighborhood people created a shrine at the spot where Oscar was murdered. We crafted a sign that read simply, "Oscar Torres Presente!" People artfully arranged candles, flowers, rosaries, a statue of Our Lady of Guadalupe, the flag of Mexico, and a big teddy bear around the sign. The shrine drew several nightly vigils during the week prior to Oscar's funeral Mass. We still have vivid memories of Francisco pouring water over the blood-stained concrete as he attempted to rub out the stain with his bare hands. And we still grieve with Ernestine, remembering her piercing wails as she prayed at Oscar's casket just before the funeral Mass. Her cry was the cry of a woman in hard labor.

July 16, 2014, would have been Oscar's sixteenth birthday. I remember his father came to the house. He thanked us for helping to raise the funds required to send Oscar's body back to San. Luis Potosi, Mexico, his birthplace, for burial. He was most grateful for our participation in creating and maintaining the shrine and asked if he could put a permanent cross or plaque by our house. We were distributing food bags that day and shared one with the Torres family. To celebrate Oscar's birthday, we were able to offer the family two dozen of Carol Rosen's freshly baked peanut butter cookies. Carol bakes cookies for the soup kitchen every week, and these beauties had just arrived. ¡Feliz cumpleanos! Happy birthday, Oscar!

Oscar's was the second murder in our alley in the last nine years. In 2005 Sam "Scooby" Umstead had been gunned down in similar fashion. We commemorated these two brothers with a simple hand-painted sign commemorating their lives. The sign is planted behind our Stone of Hope. We renamed Boyd Street (actually an alley), the Alley of Tears.

I looked it up: Baltimore really is "the city that bleeds" as some pundits put it. Local politicians detest it when people view Baltimore through the lens of the HBO series *The Wire*. But we are witnesses to the truth. In the last forty-five years, 11,582 people have been murdered in Baltimore City. During the 1990s, 3,204 brothers and sisters were killed, almost one per day. To put this in perspective, the 11,582 deaths are almost double the number of U.S. combat deaths in Iraq and Afghanistan combined.

We can grow weary doing this work. Yes, we can.

Recently we have thought it best to cut back on some of the work and reflect upon the recent violence. From our perspective, Baltimore is a dying city. Charm City stopped making contributions to the common good a long time ago. Instead we embrace ball parks, luxury hotels, casino gambling, and an economy that only benefits the 1 percent at the expense of the 99 percent. For this embrace we get the violence of poverty. We get despair. We create people who become angry and start swinging at everything and sometimes at everyone. We see people looking for work that has disappeared. And they too are growing wearier.

We realize now even more deeply that our work is not just preparing and serving food or providing shelter for homeless sisters and brothers. That's the easy work. The hard work is the battle against the powers and principalities that worship at the altar of violence and greed. It's necessary that we fight this battle. Even a small victory wouldn't hurt once in a while. *¡Oscar Torres, presente!*

Joy... Couragio

52

Chapter 4: Freddie Gray's Baltimore

Believe

We're probably going to end up a small city, gentrified, primarily white, primarily well-to-do. And [with a touch of bitterness] I think the rest of the United States thinks that's just fine.
—Garland Robinson, in Spike Lee's documentary, When the Levees Broke: A Requiem in Four Acts

Our so-called leaders and developers have a plan for Baltimore. It's Katrinaesque. No, we haven't been ravaged by a hurricane. Not yet. In Baltimore, sometimes known as Charm City or Harm City depending on where you live, human beings are implementing the plan. It's a simple plan really. Get the poor out of the city, and let the party begin. The Katrina hurricane was the spark in New Orleans; many poor people did not return to the Crescent City. Despite the U.S. Constitution, the prophets of Israel, the four Gospels, and elementary human compassion, many cities are attempting to make it illegal to break bread and provide nourishment to the poor in all public places.

I still remember one vivid example of this behavior. In 2000, a few days before Christmas, Baltimore police handcuffed me and three other activists at City Hall Plaza. We were distributing sandwiches to a group of hungry people, an activity that had been welcomed for years. Martin O'Malley, the mayor at the time, decided that this activity would no longer be tolerated. His reasoning was that groups like ours leave garbage behind, causing rat infestation, or encourage aggressive panhandling in front of City Hall. Fortunately, the press who covered City Hall saw what was happening and began asking questions.

O'Malley, or some city official, decided it would be embarrassing to Baltimore if people were arrested for sharing food with hungry people during the holiday season. Our plastic handcuffs were cut off, and we distributed the rest of the sandwiches.

In Baltimore we've already blown up all high rise public housing units, and low rise public housing is becoming a memory. The federal government is getting out of the housing business. Privatization is all the rage. The free market will provide. The lamb is now the lion's prey.

In our city the lack of affordable housing, an educational system that is a cruel joke, the scarcity of meaningful work, and unjust wages for service workers have created a human-made hurricane. Quite simply, the people of too-much-wealth are protected and encouraged by the state through tax breaks, deals with developers, and poorly regulated financial institutions. They are creating a new Baltimore for themselves. And the developers always promise that the community being developed will benefit immeasurably. This community is, quite often, increasingly composed of relative newcomers, generally better educated and more affluent than the people they are displacing.

The latest subsidy (2016) gives $17.5 million of Baltimore residents' tax dollars to Wexford Science & Technology, the real estate firm developing an expansion of the University of Maryland's BioPark. This gift is called a TIF, Tax Increment Financing subsidy, which gives Wexford long-term financing at low rates and absolves it from paying property taxes for a period of time. It is important to note that the blocks around BioPark, which is just a short walk from Viva House, are changing rapidly. Nearby public housing high rises were demolished in the 1990s, and land surrounding it is gradually being cleared. Indeed the community adjacent to BioPark will benefit from the development, but it will be a new community that is well-heeled financially. It will be win-win for developers and new residents and lose-lose for current residents, who will not be able to afford higher rents or higher sale prices.

This kind of redevelopment plan could have been neatly woven into Mayor O'Malley's BELIEVE campaign. BELIEVE was a public relations campaign someone dreamed up to promote the city. Signs with the word "BELIEVE" could be seen everywhere—on city trucks, on all public and many private buildings, on benches, t-shirts, and even garbage cans. But where do we put our belief? In the state? In the institutional church? In the banks? In corporations? This campaign had nothing to do with believing in Jesus, the human one. It was not about believing in our solidarity with the poor, or in the common good, or in respecting the Golden Rule.

What was it then? Where are we anyway?

Long ago our society lost a fundamental understanding of the common good and the necessity for human solidarity. Life in our neighborhood, Sowebo, reflects this loss in the extreme. Life here is socially unjust, economically unworkable, and remarkably dysfunctional. In Sowebo very few people have finished high school, and only a handful have college degrees. Over 40 percent of our houses are abandoned, and our unemployment rate exceeds 50 percent.

Buying and selling drugs is essential to Sowebo's economy. We have chosen to wage war on drugs rather than treat addiction as a public health problem. We are told that surveillance will protect us. So we are under constant surveillance. Cameras surround us. PODS (portable overt digital surveillance) cameras record our movements. Blue light cameras are permanently mounted on light poles. They flash on and off all day and all night. They say we can be watched from police headquarters.

Imagine! BELIEVE! Homeland Security dumps big bucks into Baltimore, and our politicians buy expensive cameras. They want us to believe in state-sanctioned surveillance, which leads inevitably to state-sanctioned violence and more and more jail cells. It's like asking us to believe in a New Orleans levee.

So, where are we? So is this Baghdad? Or Fallujah? Or Beirut?

Whenever they feel like it, the authorities roll out generator-powered flood lights and light up entire blocks all night long. We are not consulted. Can our children sleep? Does the blinding light create even more tension? Who cares? Just BELIEVE in us. Just between you and me, this entire BELIEVE campaign is similar to the Guinness Stout commercial, which encourages us to believe in the quality of the beer. In truth, it is probably better to believe in the stout. At least it has some protein.

So, where are we? Is this Kabul? Or Darfur? Where are we?

Maryland is the second wealthiest state in the union. But one of four Baltimoreans lives in poverty. Of the 236 areas in the U.S. that are similar in size to Baltimore, only two areas, one in the Bronx and one in Texas, are in worse shape economically. So, where are we?

Baltimore's population continues to decline, but is leveling off. At this point, there is no place left to go if you're not making it. So you stay in Baltimore. Only 622,000 people currently live in Baltimore, and 25 percent are not making it. In all probability, they will not make it, given the current economic arrangement. So for these folks we have jail. One year, during Martin O'Malley's mayoral administration, one hundred thousand people were arrested. The poor take up most of the jail space, and too many arrests are for what are termed quality of life offenses. Roughly translated, these crimes are loitering or peeing in public or being in the wrong place or just having no place to go. The real crimes, the crimes that the powerful inflict on the powerless—unemployment, unaffordable or uninhabitable housing, woeful miseducation—are never addressed.

So where are we? Is this Abu Ghraib? Or Guantanamo? Or a CIA Black Hole? So what are we to BELIEVE?

Among cities with populations over five hundred thousand, Baltimore is the second most violent city. Only Detroit has more violent crime. For almost two decades our murder rate has exceeded forty murders per one hundred thousand people.

In 2015, 344 murders were reported, and Baltimore set a record of fifty-five murders per one hundred thousand people. And among 239 school districts with total enrollments greater than twenty-five thousand, Baltimore is the most racially segregated. Hyper-segregation they say.

So where are we? Is this ground zero? Are we enemy combatants or something?

This nation and this city have been doing the wrong things for so long people have begun to believe they are right. Then they say we're crazy because we expose the madness. So is extraordinary rendition part of our future?

So what are we to BELIEVE?

How 'bout Dem Os, Hon!

Baltimore has two new stadiums, one for football, one for baseball. It's amazing. There's always money for bread and circuses.

The Governor rants and raves.
The mayor he just sits,
Clueless but reading.
Developer Willard Hackerman, he just laughs and
Counts the gold
All the way to the right field wall.
But, hey, how 'bout dem Os, hon!
Public space . . . a memory.
But, have we got private . . .
Festival marketplaces,
Holiday, policed shopping, Mall thralls,
Consumerism a-go-go.
Big sky boxes,
Higher, higher, higher,
Like the rents and the wounds.
But, hey, how 'bout dem Os, hon!

Meanwhile,
The kids on the street
Not coming home at night.
Time on the hand
No work for their hands. Schoolboys carry guns, not books.
Metal detectors, no books to read.

Libraries a-gone-gone.
But, hey, how 'bout dem Os, hon!

The walls are up . . .
Right, Center, Left
Great stadium, divided city.
Us. Them.
Have plenty, want more
vs.
Have nothing, no trickling down. Work. Scarce.
Part-time, part-pay, low-pay No-pay.
But, hey, how 'bout dem Os, hon!

The joke in Charm City:
The difference between preschool kids and school kids is simple . . .
the preschoolers lack the coordination
to pull the trigger.
But, hey, how 'bout dem Os, hon!

Oh, one more thing. We'll see to it,
We'll guarantee it that the poor will
always, always, always be here.
Wait! baby,
that ball is
going, going, baby,
that ball is gone!
But, hey, how 'bout dem Os, hon!

Name that Hippo!

The citizens agreed never to mention this hippo and never call it by name, so while the creature grew larger each day, occupying more and more space, no one ever pointed to it, and no one ever named it. A prophetess warned the people that they had better name the hippo and then do something about its insatiable appetite. If they kept avoiding the obvious, she said, soon the hippopotamus would take over, crush every citizen, and destroy the room. The people did nothing. And quite predictably, the hippo went wild, devouring all the people and leveling the room.
—Paraphrase of a timely parable written by Ed Loring, a member of the Open Door Community in Atlanta

There's a hippo in one of America's large rooms. It's the sickness of our cities. As it grows larger and more dangerous each day, it is crucial that it be named and that its alarming growth be addressed.

We have experienced this sickness every day in the Viva House neighborhood. In an area less than a mile in every direction from the house, we see things that assault body and soul. A low-intensity war is being waged. Evictions are daily outrages. A family's possessions are piled in the street. People are publicly humiliated. They lose their meager belongings and part of their lives.

Everyone faces the reality of brutal violence. Murder in our homes. Murder on our front stoops. Murder on our corners. Drive-by shootings are commonplace. And, given the firepower available to anyone strong enough to pull a trigger, innocent people are butchered. This violence runs top to bottom. The big boys in the U.S. Pentagon slaughter people in Iraq. Then the carnage trickles down to youngsters in Baltimore as youngsters kill each other. Chickens do come home to roost. Residents of our neighborhood are on the bottom pile of a caste system. After studying data from the 1990 census, we discovered that 17 percent of abandoned houses in the city are in our neighborhood. Fifty-five percent of our children live below the poverty line.

Half of our people between the ages of sixteen and sixty-four are not part of the work force. Only 42 percent of our neighbors above the age of twenty-five are high school graduates. Thirty-nine percent of our teenagers are not in school and are not high school graduates. In a typical year, we have a murder every sixteen days; a woman is raped every seven days; we have one armed robbery and one assault every other day. And that is just what is reported.

We have been told repeatedly that Baltimore is in the middle of a renaissance. For several decades self-appointed urban saviors and some politicians have told us repeatedly what they have won for us—dead-end, nonunion, minimum-wage, part-time jobs. These saviors know that such jobs could not replace the one hundred thousand manufacturing jobs lost in the last two decades. They are aware of the huge high school dropout rate and the work force gap in Baltimore, where fully a fourth of our citizens lack the education and skills required to perform anything but poorly paid jobs with no future.

In naming this hippo and addressing its growth, we have to consider the greed factor. Baltimore *Evening Sun* reporter Joan Jacobson did some of that naming in an article documenting the number of development projects launched in Baltimore with government (taxpayer) loans that will never be repaid, many already written off by city finance officials. "Greed" was never mentioned by those civic leaders and developers defending the practice, but it should have been.

It is time to name the hippopotamus. Baltimore is nothing more than one large room, and some of us are watching the hippo expand each day. The animal wants more space. When it finally goes on a rampage, it will devour everyone and destroy everything. We'll lose City Hall and what's left of public housing. Harborplace and the stadiums will collapse. Republicans and Democrats will feel the sting. The hippo will destroy both those who hoard the bread and those who beg for the crumbs.

Surfers and Swimmers

Here on Crocker Street, we feel as if we have stepped into a morass of problems of such depth and gravity that they make our meager gifts of bread and coffee seem about as helpful and effective as a Popsicle in hell.
—Jeff Dietrich, Los Angeles Catholic Worker

Jeff Dietrich is speaking a painful truth. Our soup kitchens and food pantries, our temporary shelters and health centers for street people, our Thanksgiving dinners, Christmas baskets, and food banks seem about as useful as his Popsicle.

Dietrich reminds us, moreover, that the Hebrew word for hell is *gehenna*, literally "garbage dump." So, for the most part, we offer the poor Popsicles in Baltimore's garbage dumps, those streets and alleys where people are not making it, where they might never make it.

In hell the Popsicle melts rapidly. It does not quench thirst. Instead, its temporary sweetness only makes the thirsty more thirsty.

When we began Viva House, Dorothy Day reminded us that soup kitchens and food pantries were necessary in times of crisis. They were not meant to be permanent fixtures. The steaming soup bowls, crusty casseroles, and folding cots were only intended to provide immediate relief. People were not meant to live in a perpetual state of crisis. In the late 1960s and through most of the 1970s, most of the folks who visited us were single men, usually over forty and only temporarily down and out.

Now there are women and children, legions of them, living hand to mouth, doubled-up in homes, waiting for the bureaucrats to announce the beginning of the "homeless season" when the government provides a little more temporary shelter for homeless people. The government believes that it is only a short season, running from mid-November until the end of March.

The future isn't hopeful. Temporary aid has become the permanent solution. In East Baltimore people are proud to announce that ten thousand Thanksgiving dinners were served. It is common for people to be arrested at City Hall for demanding the same things people were demanding a decade ago—a few more beds, a few more crumbs.

In a Christmas reflection, the late Thomas Merton described places like Baltimore as "demented inns" where Jesus is not welcome, where the "rich are filled with more things and the poor are turned away empty." Some studies point out that professional and research jobs in such fields as finance, medicine, engineering, and law comprise 40 percent of Baltimore's total employment. At the same time, we have lost thousands of blue-collar and unionized jobs. The Port of Baltimore is an example. Its cargo volume has decreased significantly, and fewer employees are needed to unload the ships.

The factories and mills where people used to earn good wages are now idle, repurposed as trendy condos or simply torn down. We have become, as Berkeley economist Robert Reich wrote, a city of surfers and swimmers. Many of the surfers, those in professional and research jobs, are riding the waves, splashing the shores of the Inner Harbor and nearby gold coast. They furnish their condominiums stylishly, entertain in them lavishly, and life is grand. The swimmers, those who are a paycheck away from the streets or are already on the streets, are beginning to drown. The harbor is polluted for them. If they can get one of the few available jobs, it will likely be in retail sales or in the tourist industry. In short, it will be serving the surfers.

The sad fact is that many of our citizens have become expendable labor. They are not needed in the present economic arrangement. So they end up swimming laps, banging into one wall only to turn around and bang into another one.

We must examine where we are going. Our inability to humanize technology is brutalizing us. People are disconnected from the earth itself. Children are parceled out to under-funded day care centers so that parents can work and tread water. Then we wonder why many families are disjointed and why John and Mary can't read or why they become emotional basket cases. There's no talk about ending the homeless crisis with permanent housing or providing the hungry with the wherewithal to feed themselves.

Each time we serve a plate of food or assemble a bag of food at Viva House, we know we are swimming against the tide. We need a maximum as well as a minimum wage. We need more than Popsicles and temporary measures.

Zero Tolerance

Zero Tolerance is a policy enacted during Mayor Martin O'Malley's administration. The result: one hundred thousand arrests and growing tension between the police and the people.

Life springs from death,
and from the graves
of the unemployed
and the spit-upon women and men
spring revolutionary people.
The defenders of the aristocracy
have worked in secret and in the open.
They think they can control people
with high-tech surveillance cameras
and zero tolerance laws.
They think they can lock up
half the poor and
intimidate the other half.
They think they know everything and
have foreseen everything.
But the fools, the fools, the fools!
They have left us half-starved, woefully
undereducated children.
They have left us evicted neighbors,
and sisters and brothers who
sleep in open weather, some even frozen to death.
And, while Baltimore ignores these people,
her neighborhoods will
never
be at peace.

—Inspired by Padraig Pearse, a leader of Ireland's Easter Uprising of 1916

Freddie Gray

Everyone's struggle for justice usually begins with one's own suffering.
—Bernadette Devlin McAliskey, civil rights leader in Ireland

Why did Baltimoreans rise up after the death of Freddie Gray while in police custody?

Why does it appear that we learned nothing after the 1968 Baltimore riots?

Why does the inner city continue to get the shaft, while corporate Baltimore is all aglow and flourishing?

Why are all our local police being militarized, and why are we creating a surveillance state par excellence?

At least let us speak honestly with one another. Lies and mythology only produce greater disasters. After the 1968 Baltimore riots, the officials and the elites huddled together and with great zeal agreed that there must be only one Baltimore. They got to work immediately and over the next forty-seven years, the officials, the bankers, and the developers did indeed build one Baltimore. We got festival shopping at Harborplace. Our taxes paid for a baseball stadium and a football stadium. We now have more hotels than we need and a convention center. Developers have gentrified the neighborhoods of Canton, Harbor East, Federal Hill, and Locust Point. An obscene casino recently opened adjacent to the stadiums. If you lived on the shores of the Inner Harbor, you became the One Baltimore. We, the inner city residents, are supposed to be grateful for this collection of golden calves.

After Freddie Gray's death in the custody of the Baltimore police, the chickens came home to roost. The collective heart of the disenfranchised poured out its disgust with the status quo. No more! No more! The cup of endurance flowed over just like it did in '68. Police brutality and constant surveillance had to end. As journalist and activist Chris Hedges points out so clearly, our black sisters and brothers have been dealing with continual violence since the first slave ship landed centuries ago. The cycle runs thus: slavery, segregation, share cropping, convict leasing, Jim Crow, lynching, urban decay, extreme poverty, unrelenting unemployment, racism, and prison.

If you lived in the other Baltimore, Freddie Gray's Baltimore, the often violent Baltimore, the recent uprising was expected. In fact, we often wondered what took so long. You cannot have a peaceful city when at least one-third of the population is disregarded, undereducated, repeatedly jailed by a zero toleration policy, and continuing to lose hope. You cannot have a livable city when a major source of income in poor neighborhoods is the drug trade. You cannot sit back and allow absolute violence. In the last forty-seven years almost twelve thousand Baltimoreans have been murdered. In the months since the riot curfew was lifted, a murder occurred every day.

In West Baltimore it is even more violent now than during the riots following Gray's death.

While the Renaissance Baltimore was taking shape, the real Baltimore lost over one hundred and fifty thousand blue collar jobs. Manufacturing jobs were becoming nonexistent. During the years William Donald Schaefer was mayor (1971–1987), one hundred and seventy thousand people packed up and left the city. Then, between 1990 and 2010, another one hundred and fourteen thousand citizens slipped away. Sweet Jesus, please tell us how this mess could ever have been called a renaissance? We are left with six hundred and twenty-two thousand people, and a good third of them will probably never work a job that pays anything resembling a just, livable family wage. There can only be One Baltimore if all its citizens have work that contributes to the common good and pays a family wage. Tourism, ballgames, and a casino hardly fit the bill.

Increasingly safety nets are being cut. Public housing is becoming a memory. And so-called market rents are far greater than poor folks can afford. So, enter the drug trade big time. Enter a militarized, even more poorly trained police. Enter an increasing and bloody homicide rate. Enter more arrests with no bail. And you have a recipe for even more uprisings.

Our good friend the late Bill O'Connor always insisted that everything in the universe is related to everything else in the universe. This relationship is most evident in the chasm dividing rich and poor. Thus, enormous wealth in the pockets of a tiny few means empty pockets for most of the people in the world. It means 1 percent vs. 99 percent. It means extravagant excess vs unfathomable suffering. In Baltimore, as everywhere, everything is related; Baltimore is a reflection of this inequality.

At some point we must replace the loss of manufacturing jobs. We cannot allow corporations to escape paying taxes by hiding wealth all over the world and by exploiting millions of workers in underdeveloped countries. We must have an answer for robots, obsolescence, weather chaos, and workers whose labor has become expendable. We cannot pit Asian workers against U.S. workers. Technology has developed faster than anything we could ever have imagined, and we must deal with it so that no person is considered obsolete or expendable. It is a challenge to our compassion and imagination.

The other big hippo in the room is violence. Face it, the U.S. is the most violent nation in the world. Our military budget is larger than the next ten largest military budgets in the world combined, including those of Russia, China, the United Kingdom, France, and Saudi Arabia. We have spent seventy trillion dollars on a nuclear arsenal since 1945, and we are the only nation to launch nuclear weapons on another country. We engage in torture, we operate "black sites," including at Guantanamo Bay Naval Base, and we have invaded Iraq and Afghanistan. And this is just the most recent violence. Our country was founded on genocide as we butchered Native Americans and took their land. The violence has continued ever since. By word and act we teach violence. We tell our youth that violence solves problems, big and little, both worldwide and on the local corner.

The riots following Freddie Gray's death cost Baltimore more than twenty million dollars. Six cops have been indicted on serious charges. Non-corporate store owners, who were robbed or burned out and who carried no insurance, will probably not recover. The consensus in our neighborhood is that there will be more Freddie Grays, more Michael Browns, more Eric Garners, more Tamir Rices. And the U.S. will continue to raise hell anywhere and everywhere. The banks will flourish. Austerity will be imposed as a solution to the resulting financial crises. We will be assured that our drones are even more accurate and that filling our prisons is necessary for the economy. Soon it will appear as if nothing happened.

So what does the Catholic Worker have to offer? Simple. Just stand there! Don't surrender to the long loneliness. Resist the filthy rotten system. Do the works of mercy. Pray while you refuse to go along. Pray while you're doing the work. And laugh. Hell yes, laugh!

Glory be to God for dappled things—

Pied Beauty
Gerard Manley Hopkins, S.J.

COURAGE

" **LOVE** without **COURAGE** and **WISDOM**
is sentimentality, as with the ordinary church member.
   COURAGE without **LOVE** and **WISDOM**
is foolhardiness, as with the ordinary soldier.
   WISDOM without **LOVE** and **COURAGE**
is cowardice, as with the ordinary intellectual.
Therefore, one who has **LOVE**, **COURAGE** and **WISDOM**
is one in a million who moves the world,
as with Jesus, Buddha, Gandhi "and **Dorothy**.

      -from Ammon Hennacy

Dorothy Day 1897-1980

68

Chapter 5: Couragio

Lazarus Cries Out

Modern society calls the beggars bums and panhandlers and gives them the bum's rush. But, the Greeks used to say that people in need are, in fact, the ambassadors of the gods.
—*Peter Maurin,* Easy Essays

If you take a few minutes and reread the parable, the Rich Man and Lazarus (Luke 16:19-31), you clearly hear the cry of the poor. Lazarus, the poor man, is covered with festering sores, and he cries out for the scraps from the rich man's table. At the soup kitchen we hear this cry each day. It's loud. It's clear. It's enunciated unashamedly.

For the most part, no one listens to Lazarus or to the folks lined up at the soup kitchens all over Baltimore. We pretend not to notice the suffering of the thousands caged in our prisons or those fifty thousand Baltimoreans broken apart with addictions. But Lazarus keeps crying out. Thank God for that. He is our only hope if we want to keep our sanity and our humanity.

Clarence Jordan of the Koinonia Community in Georgia tells us that the Greek word for beggar is *pochos* and the etymology of that word is "spit." Lazarus is not just a poor member of our community. He is a person who is spit upon. When presidents, governors, mayors, and members of groups like the Greater Baltimore

Committee plug their ears and refuse to hear Lazarus, all of us are in deep trouble. Lazarus forces us to confront all the problems that plague Baltimore. And at the core of these problems is how do we treat Lazarus? Do we welcome him, or do we give him the bum's rush?

No matter what U.S. city you are in, the agenda is the same. Any potentially profitable section of downtown or any area deemed ripe for upscale development is seized by a legalism known as eminent domain. Any business or residence that is in the way is torn down. Big developers know what is best for the city and, of course, for themselves. So you get a stadium here, a Starbucks there, a few trendy restaurants and hotels over there, and some loft apartments or condos up there.

No one cares what Lazarus thinks. Consequently, a huge ditch is dug. A wide gulf separates Lazarus from those climbing to the top rungs of the ladder. Then those same people blow up Lazarus's public housing and move him wherever they choose or leave him to fend for himself. Then they attempt to privatize whatever remaining options they choose. If there is any resistance, well, that's why we keep building more prisons.

We need to give Lazarus a proper voice. After all, in Luke's parable it is Lazarus who ends up in the bosom of Abraham: "Rock my soul in the bosom of Abraham"—that's about Lazarus. The rich man ends up begging Lazarus for water while he stews in Hades. Let's suppose that Lazarus forms a new committee. He gathers a group of his brothers and sisters, the spit-upon people, and they form the Baltimore Committee for the Least of These. Then this committee makes recommendations: The Spit-Upon People cry out!

On a Union Harbor

We need to think about organizing more unions in Baltimore, and wouldn't it be grand if Baltimore could be known as the city where all the workers were organized into one big union. The return of the IWW, the International Workers of the World. Janitors, nurses, dishwashers, doctors, lawyers, laborers, domestics, teachers, hotel employees, and so on would form One Big Union. And this union would grow and extend beyond the Chesapeake Bay. We need to understand that an injury to a worker in Malaysia or Chiapas or Baltimore would be an injury to all workers and thus a cause for action.

Clearly, we need bread and roses. We need just, family-enriching wages. Think about it. If the U.S. minimum wage kept pace with the pay of corporate CEOs since 1960, it would now be $57 per hour or $2,280 per week or $118,560 per year.

On Transportation

We don't care about high-speed, high-priced maglev trains. We're more concerned about getting to work quickly and easily in Baltimore. In fact, we want free mass transit traveling in every direction.

Let's begin phasing out the private cars. Let's stop the construction of ugly parking lots and garages. Let's open up the city for cyclists and walkers. In the summer let's ban private cars altogether.

On Prison

Why have we locked up two million of our brothers and sisters nationwide? For every one hundred thousand U.S. citizens, 668 are in our jails and prisons, and we keep constructing new cells daily. Why do we put young kids in adult jails or ship them off to boot camps? They return to their same neighborhoods bitter, depressed, traumatized people.

What kind of madness have we embraced? Nationwide, seven of ten prisoners are substance abusers, four of ten are drug offenders, seven of ten did not finish high school, one of ten suffers from a mental illness.

We need an open dialogue between victims and victimizers. We need to restore communities nonviolently. Jail just adds more violence to the raging fire. So, we make a suggestion. Let's all read Marc Mauer's book, *Race to Incarcerate: The Sentencing Project*, and Jim Consedine's *Restorative Justice: Healing the Effects of Crime*. Both books offer insights that could help us climb out of the punishment trough. No more three strikes and you're out. No more death penalty.

On Healthy Neighborhoods

Quoting my friend, Dan Berrigan, S.J., let's not embark on a health care model "where the powerful mock the powerless with games of triage" and where we only lend a hand to so-called healthy neighborhoods. The result of such a policy is that in saving the saved, we bury the weak. Let's lend a hand to the people the wealthy have buried in the ditch.

For starters, let's put at least one public health care worker in every census tract. Their responsibilities would include all facets of public health, physical, social, psychological, and spiritual. We would then get a first-hand knowledge of the presence of lead paint and housing code violations, people suffering from addiction, people with AIDS and other chronic illnesses, people overwhelmed by utility bills or high rents, people in need of childcare or of mental health care. The list is endless but not hopeless. Then we channel resources to the needs.

And on and on and on—you complete the recommendations.

We've got to fill in the gap that divides the rich from the poor. Primarily, it dehumanizes the rich. The rich have to climb out of their bulldozers and begin filling in the hole. Lazarus will not keep quiet.

Love, Wisdom, and Courage: Commencement Address
Given at Friends School of Baltimore High School Graduation • 2001

Lifelong pacifist-anarchist Ammon Hennacy provided us with a valuable insight. He wrote: "Love without wisdom and courage is sentimentality, as with the ordinary church member. Wisdom without love and courage is cowardice, as with the ordinary intellectual. Courage without love and wisdom is foolhardiness, as with the ordinary soldier."

Therefore, a high school graduate who possesses or seeks to pos-

sess, love, wisdom, and courage is that one in a million who will move the world, as did Gandhi or Mother Jones or Isaiah or Buddha or Helen Keller or Jesus or Malcolm X or Martin Luther King, Jr. or Dorothy Day.

Think about it: love, wisdom, courage in action.

You want to take these virtues with you to college, to future worksites, to future neighborhoods, to future relationships and families. And you'll need all three. The world is upside down. Baltimore is upside down. My god, we've left you young people quite a mess. You'll need all the love, wisdom, and courage you can find, now more than ever.

A native chieftain on a small island in the South Pacific observed (quite wisely, I think) that there are only two societies in the whole wide world. One is the society of money; the other is the society of people. For those who are weighted down with an overabundance of possessions, this division is a gross oversimplification. But if you are one of the poorest of the poor, the condition endured by most of the world's population, we might note, it is a valid and truthful division.

After this evening's graduation celebration, each of you will go a separate way, and each of you will be faced with a lifelong choice: do you want to live in the society of money or the society of people? And don't kid yourself. You can't have it both ways. There is a conflict between money and people. You can't serve money and people at the same time. One brings blindness and paralysis; the other illuminates and forces you to act.

If you choose the society of money (and there is a great temptation to make that choice), you agree to accept some dangerous things:

You accept the god of shopping,

the god of the survival of the fittest,

the gods of metal, nuclear weapons, depleted uranium.

You accept the absurd reality that there are more shopping malls than high schools in the U.S.

You accept U.S. sanctions in Iraq where forty-five thousand chil-

dren under the age of five die each month, and you accept the U.S. military budget. Currently at $350 billion, it is twenty-two times larger than the combined military budgets of the seven countries identified as enemy by the Pentagon. And this military madness is rooted in our insatiable appetite for oil and economic dominance in the world. Sadly, we have spilled blood and are prepared to spill more so that we can drive our cars as often as we wish.

You accept local laws that harass and attempt to control the poor and homeless on a daily basis. Move on! Move out! Don't share meals in front of City Hall! Get out of Harborplace! Don't sit in front of the library! In fact, just get out of Baltimore! And you are beset with callous indignities like fining people for begging without permits or insisting that beggars stand at least three feet away from the person they are begging from.

You accept a grossly distorted and unbalanced distribution of wealth. Worldwide, three hundred and fifty-eight billionaires control 45 percent of the per capita income of the world. In the U.S., the richest 10 percent of the population has 70 percent of the wealth; the bottom 40 percent, less than 1 percent. So hypothetically, if total wealth in the U.S. was just one hundred dollars and our total population was just 100 people, the 10 richest people would control seventy dollars, and the other 90 people would have only thirty dollars left to share. Actually, the 20 poorest people would have only pocket change at best.

Then there is the society of people. If you choose to live in this society, be prepared. The road is not paved. It's filled with treacherous ditches and land mines. And you won't get rich in this society. This is where you'll need love, wisdom, and courage in large doses. In the society of people, the land, the air, and the sea are all sources of life. They are not for sale, and they are not to be wasted or polluted. They are sacred and meant to be shared for the common good.

In the society of people, love is understood in the concrete, the here and now. There is nothing abstract about it. There is no such thing as the deserving and undeserving poor. Love simply means that all people are one and are entitled to justice and all the necessities of life. If one person suffers injury, all people suffer injury. There are no "isms" in the society of people. Racism, sexism, classism are all abolished. Forgiveness, not revenge, is the common practice. The Oklahoma City bomber Timothy McVeigh is forgiven, as is former Nebraska senator and Vietnam War veteran Bob Kerrey. Both men killed innocent people. Both men were trained to kill by the Pentagon. But we forgive them both. In the society of people, capital punishment and executions cease to exist, and nuclear warheads are rendered useless forever.

In the society of people, true wisdom underlies action, and common sense prevails. We realize that reverence for people is the beginning of wisdom. Thus, it is common sense to understand that drug addiction is a serious illness that demands treatment. We do not build more prisons then crowd them with addicts. No, we meet the problem head on, always realizing that helping an addict recover might take years and years.

Wisdom tells us that policing tactics and zero tolerance policies don't achieve public safety. You have public safety when all the public is safe. You have public safety when all our schools offer the same quality of education that Friends School provides. You have public safety when every family has safe, decent, affordable housing, proper nutrition, and health care. You have public safety when you have full employment with jobs that pay living family wages. Throwing more and more money to the police is literally throwing it down a bottomless sewer. You don't get public safety; you get tension, fear, ignorance, and hatred.

Finally, you need courage. It is the most important virtue. If you lack courage, you can't practice any of the other virtues. You need courage to practice love and wisdom. Courage involves risk. You start to realize, as did the theologian and anti-Nazi Dietrich Bonhoeffer, that "not only do you have to bandage the victims caught under the wheel, you have to jam a stick in the wheel." You have to clog the wheel and prevent it from crushing anyone else. Inevitably, this means conflict with the rulers, the powerful, the wealthy. And you will always be tempted to flee the society of people for the apparent safety of the society of money.

The hope is that each graduate of Friends School, Class of 2001, will take a long, hard look at society and examine the choices in front of them. Think about love, wisdom, and courage. Be that one in a million who will move the world. What we need is a society where it is easier for people to be good.

What about the People in Steerage?

I'm not a big user of the computer and still prefer newspapers, magazines, good books, and thoughtful, hand-written letters. But the reality is that the technological current rushes forward, and people expect you to read and answer e-mails, search the web, et cetera, et cetera, et cetera.

We receive e-mails from various sources, and many are both timely and important. I saved a few of them over the past months. Frank Cordaro of the Des Moines Catholic Worker and our Baltimore friend Max Obuszewski do a fantastic job of finding articles from newspapers, speeches, and the like and sending them to us over the internet. In many ways they are my newspaper. I share with you a summary of two recent e-mails from these folks and add short reflections.

From Max Obuszewski: In 1849 the Sisters of Charity, the community of my sister, Pat, founded St. Vincent's Hospital in Greenwich Village. The hospital was forced into bankruptcy and closed its doors at the end of April 2010. This means that there is not a single Catholic general hospital in New York City. When I was a kid, there were many of them.

New York Times reporter Anemona Hartocollis summed up this closing by quoting Sr. Miriam Kevin Phillips, a nurse and senior vice president for mission at St. Vincent's. She said, "St. Vincent's was inexorably defeated by its devotion to the poor and by the transformation of Greenwich Village from a home for immigrants and the working class to a neighborhood filled with wealthy people who were drawn to more prestigious academic medical centers."

Sr. Kevin also noted that St. Vincent's served survivors of the *Titanic* sinking and the 9/11 attacks on the World Trade Center. Her comment about the *Titanic* survivors makes a lasting impression: "The Sisters of Charity wired the rescue ship, the *Carpathia*, that St. Vincent's ambulances would be waiting at the dock but would take only passengers from steerage. The Sisters knew," she stated, "that the rich passengers would be taken care of." They always are.

Reflection

We're told that one of ten people living on Manhattan Island is a millionaire. Harlem is changing fast. The Bowery has changed. The wealthy want the island. It's like Columbus all over again. Manhattan, my birthplace, has been rediscovered. The moneyed folks are taking over a land that is already inhabited. Where do the earlier inhabitants go? What happens to the sick poor? Who cares? The same thing is happening in many cities. The unwritten plan is quite simple: those who have the most want our cities smaller, whiter, and, of course, richer. They think this will make our cities safer. We see it happening in Baltimore too. Manufacturing jobs have disappeared. Unskilled folks can flip the burgers, sweep the streets, clean the toilets, and make the hotel beds. But that's it. Foreclosures continue. Every rent goes higher, higher. And the poor wander from job to joblessness, from one inadequate home or shelter to another. Capitalism doesn't need them anymore.

For the rich everything is hunky-dory. Labor unions are decimated, and the ever-present and always well-fed military gobbles up half the plate. It is mind boggling that so many of our citizens refuse to comprehend that an endless war policy—Iraq, Afghanistan, Pakistan, maybe Iran and North Korea too—eats us alive economically and spiritually.

So, we stand at the dock with Sr. Kevin and ask: "What about the people in steerage?"

Saying No

What is a rebel? A person who says "No!"
—Albert Camus

Frank Cordaro sent us several e-mail articles written by Chris Hedges, former New York Times foreign correspondent and Harvard Divinity School student. Hedges has been greatly influenced by the moral philosopher Albert Camus. In the face of runaway capitalism and immoral warfare, Hedges sees signs of hope in those citizens who revolt and who put their bodies under the wheels, gears, and levers of the odious machine of capitalism. "The rebel," he concludes, "is not concerned with self-promotion or public opinion. . . . In fact," he adds, "the rebel is beholden to a moral commitment that makes it impossible to stand with the power elite." The rebel knows what St. Augustine knew: "Hope has two beautiful daughters, anger and courage. Anger at the way things are and courage to see that they do not remain the way they are."

Reflection

Revolt. Hope. Anger. Courage. They are related. Catholic Worker anarchist Ammon Hennacy believed that courage was the most important virtue, because without courage it is not possible to practice the other virtues. Phil Berrigan would often bid us good-bye with a comforting "couragio!"

These days keeping up one another's courage might be the most important work we can do.

It is hazardous work giving a big nonviolent "NO!" to an economy and a military that tramples the poor to an intolerable degree. It is easier to say "yes" and just go along. But it is nonviolent resistance that really makes a person human. Chris Hedges insists that "those who do not rebel in our age of totalitarian capitalism commit moral and spiritual suicide." Couragio!

Women Didn't Run

For God's sake. Tell Pope Francis. Tell all the Catholic hierarchy. The women didn't run.

When Jesus was arrested and executed by the state, his male disciples were terrified. They went into hiding. They tucked tail and ran. Some even denied they knew the victim. The so-called male virtues of courage and bravery were nowhere to be found. Their guts runneth over. How, then, did popes come to restrict the role of generations of women in the church? How did males get to be on top of a hierarchy that increasingly has little connection to the Gospel of Jesus?

Happily, not all the disciples deserted Jesus during and after his brutal murder. In his book *Binding the Strong Man: A Political Reading of Mark's Story of Jesus, Ched Myers* highlights a crucial truth. He tells us that three women, Mary of Magdala and two others, stuck with Jesus in his dying and in his rising. Their biggest fear wasn't the Roman state but moving the stone from the entrance to Jesus's tomb.

For too long Catholics have permitted the Vatican to uphold the immoral and misguided belief that ordination to the priesthood was solely the right of males. For too long we have permitted those with mitres and croziers to step on and over women.

This sexism should be viewed in the same way as we ought to view racism. Which is to say it is a "Goddamned" thing. The church hierarchy is actually saying that women have some defect, that they are outsiders, mere objects. "She's a nobody, just a woman." Not fit or worthy of ordination. Nothing in scripture supports such blasphemy against God.

By not allowing women to share equally with men in the celebration of the Eucharist, the central event of Catholic worship, the hierarchy is telling us that God made a creative error in bringing women into being.

When we know that a group or organization is openly denying African Americans or Hispanics or Native Americans full participation in communal life, many decide to boycott, to picket, to demonstrate, that is to act creatively and nonviolently against such an injustice. Since the hierarchy has denied women the right to fully share the Lord's Supper, perhaps we should consider a moratorium on the institutional Eucharist. We would not sit at an all-white table. Why should we sit passively at a table that is all male?

Many Catholic parishes have closed or will be closing. The bishops tell us that the churches have to be padlocked because there are fewer and fewer parishioners. There is a connection here: There are fewer parishioners because the people (*sensus fidelium*) see the sham of an all-male priesthood. There are also fewer priests. Meanwhile, many excellent women walk our sidewalks and alleys. Eager. Competent. Energetic. And not running away.

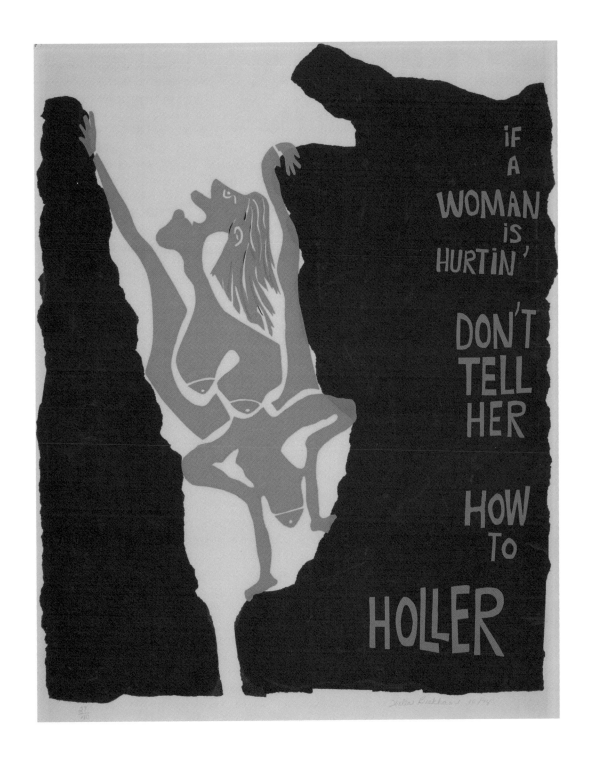

Chapter 6: Dorothy Day and the Catholic Worker

Go to the Worker

Go to the worker, especially where workers are poor; and in general, go to the poor.
—*Pope Leo XIII,* Rerum Novarum (Of Revolutionary Change)*, 1891*

When workers are striking they are following an impulse—often blind, often uninformed, but a good impulse—one could even say an inspiration of the Holy Spirit. They are trying to uphold their right to be treated not as slaves but as human beings. They are fighting for a share in the management, for their right to be considered partners in the enterprise in which they are engaged.
—*Dorothy Day,* Catholic Worker *newspaper, 1936*

Peter Maurin's comment, "Strikes don't strike me," always irritated me. Undoubtedly I need a more detailed explanation of what Peter meant, but it is my understanding that he was "unalterably opposed to industrial unionism," as James Fisher put it in *On the Irish Waterfront.*

Dorothy, on the other hand, states that striking workers could well be inspired by the Holy Spirit. Dorothy and Peter must have had heated discussions about unions and strikes.

At Viva House we've always admired Dorothy's support of unions and striking workers. We don't believe in crossing picket lines or scabbing. Strikes do strike us. From its inception, the Catholic Worker worked closely with the working class. In 1936 the CW provided hospitality for the wildcat striking merchant sailors on the New York waterfront. Fortune magazine described these seamen as the "true proletariat of the western world, the homeless, rootless and eternally unemployed."

When you support a worker's demand for justice, they start calling you "commie," "pinko," and a "god-damned red." So it was with Dorothy. And with all Catholic Workers.

In 1949 the gravediggers at Calvary Cemetery in New York City went on strike. Since my parents are buried at Calvary and since I was once a seminarian at nearby St. Joseph's Seminary, Dunwoodie, this strike is of particular interest to me. Calvary is owned by the Archdiocese of New York and New York's Cardinal Spellman ordered Dunwoodie seminarians to cross the picket line and become scabs. This they did. Why? What ever happened to Pope Leo XIII's great encyclical, *Rerum Novarum*, which supported labor unions as a means of promoting justice? Weren't the seminarians actively obeying an immoral and unjust order? Dorothy stood shoulder to shoulder with the gravediggers, not the priests-in-training, and defied the great cardinal. This same Prince of the Church would achieve even greater fame when he offered full support to the U.S. carnage in the Vietnam War.

Dorothy's involvement with Cesar Chavez and the United Farm Workers' union is perhaps the most well-known example of her heeding the call to "go to the worker." The point is that the Catholic Worker is about workers. And it should be.

When we speak with our neighbors, the men and women who share meals at Viva House, we realize that their primary concerns are meaningful work, the never-ending quest for daily bread, and a safe place to rest their weary bones and live a peaceful life with their families. All the workers of the world seek this same justice.

Each day at Viva House we "go to the worker" and offer what we have. It's quite simple. We serve a meal every Wednesday and Thursday. We distribute at least one hundred and twenty five bags of groceries every month. If we are able, we provide financial assistance for rent, gas and electric, water, and medicine bills. We view all of this as a work of justice. We are simply returning to people what is rightfully theirs.

In Sowebo, most of our neighbors are without work. The loss of more than one hundred and fifty thousand manufacturing jobs in Baltimore in the last four decades is one of the big reasons for this unemployment. A prime example is the closing of the steel mills at Sparrows Point. Forty thousand workers did hard manual labor before the closing, and they were rewarded with the dignity of work— and wages to support a family. Then, massive unemployment robbed workers of their dignity and their income. A worker without work is indeed a lonely person.

Each day we also "go to the worker" with a vision. Life should not be as difficult as it is for so many people. Every time the common good is ignored or trampled upon, it is a crime against all workers. We are meant to live together as a family, and the goods of the earth are meant to be held in common. At least that is how we see it. So, when people share meals at our tables, the art work hanging on our walls expresses some of this vision. The watercolors are messages of hope and clarity. For example:

"You poor take comfort. You rich take care. This earth was made a common treasury for everyone to share."
—Leon Rosselson

"Our problems stem from our acceptance of this filthy, rotten system."
—Dorothy Day

"Justice is what love looks like in public."
—Cornel West

Admittedly, our work and our vision are not embraced by everyone. In fact, we probably appear foolish to many. But only by embracing the concept and the truth of the common good will the loneliness and bitterness of poverty and violence be ended. We adhere to this truth and take it to the worker.

It's Gotta be the Joy

Some say working the soup kitchen
best defines the Catholic Worker.
Some say opening your home to the lonely and destitute
best defines the Catholic Worker.
Some say resisting the war makers, doing the time,
refusing to go along with the greed and violence
best define the Catholic Worker.
Some say it's all of these, knowing full well that the best we can do
is plant a few seeds, knowing full well
the harvest is a long time coming.
But, deep down, really, in our heart of hearts, we know . . .
It's gotta be the joy!
You lose joy, you lose it all.
No joy, no hope.
No joy, no endurance.
No joy, no understanding of the suffering.
No joy, no meaning to life.
No joy, and it's just another year in Guantanamo.
No joy, and we're all just doing time on the planet.
Oh, yeah—
It's gotta be the joy!

Already Acclaimed

At the November 2012 meeting of the U.S. Conference of Catholic Bishops, 230 bishops unanimously voted to advocate for the sainthood of Dorothy Day. It was reported by Catholic News Service (CNS) and Religion News Service (RNS) that these same bishops could not agree on a statement about the U.S. economy.

How is it possible that 230 bishops could unanimously endorse Dorothy's sainthood but could not make a clear, truthful, unambiguous statement about massive economic injustice and inequality in the United States? These gentlemen could easily have contacted any Catholic Worker community or simply searched any of Dorothy's writings about our fractured system of capitalism. It's a stick-up in broad daylight! What could be clearer? Presently, four hundred U.S. families, less than one percent of our population, control half of the nation's wealth.

"Saint Dorothy" could be the bishops' most reliable resource on the matter. She clearly explains the meaning of the Mystical Body, which in essence teaches that an injury to one is an injury to all. If this statement is a bit too Marxist or Wobbly for them, the bishops could easily have quoted from the Acts of the Apostles:

"The whole group of believers was united heart and soul; no one claimed for his own use anything that he had, as everything they owned was held in common." (Acts 4:32)

"None of their members was ever in want, as all who owned land or houses would sell them, and bring the money from them, to present to the apostles. It was then distributed to any members who might be in need." (Acts 4:34-35)

The clearest statements Dorothy ever made, indeed her entire life, centered on the common good and non-violence. Yes, a redistribution of wealth. Yes, the right to organize unions. Yes, the right to dignity. Yes, the right to a just family wage. Yes, the right to education. Yes, the right to health care.

And no to all war. No to all torture. No to all military drones. No to carpet bombing. No to Guantanamo. No to the Iraq and Afghanistan wars and preparation for new wars. No to more jails. No to more warfare money. The list is endless.

Dorothy's life and beliefs were clear: You do the works of mercy and you resist the works of war. Always.

If the hierarchy or any individual or group wants to declare Dorothy Day a saint, it should be done with eyes wide open. Dorothy comes with heavy commitments: a gospel of costly grace, not cheap grace. She comes with the Sermon on the Mount in heart and hands. Going to jail is part of this. Resistance to the doctrine of American exceptionalism is, too. She wasn't kidding about the idea that "love in action can be harsh and dreadful." Be prepared!

But what do we hear from the bishops? Why do they want to make Dorothy a saint? Some of the bishops shared their thoughts. Chicago's then cardinal, Francis George, promoted Dorothy's canonization by "enlisting her in the bishop's battle against the Obama administration's contraception mandate and endorsement of gay rights." Retired Washington, D.C. cardinal Theodore McCarrick thought that Dorothy would be a great help in reaching "all the people that are hard to get at—the ones who are street people, the ones who are on drugs, the ones who have had abortions . . . she was one of them."

New York City's gregarious Irish prelate, Timothy Cardinal Dolan, *primus inter pares* (first among his peers), called Dorothy Day's journey "Augustinian," saying, "She was the first to admit it: sexual immorality, there was a religious search, there was a pregnancy out of wedlock, and an abortion. Like Saul on the way to Damascus, she was radically changed and has become a saint for our time."

So what's going on? Are the bishops attempting to hijack Dorothy and make her a saint to their liking? Are they trying to use her life to support their agenda? Dorothy spoke and wrote very little about abortion, birth control, and sexual immorality. When you think about Dorothy's life and work, these aren't the first issues you ponder. You can make an analogy to Willie Mays. When they enshrined Willie Mays in the National Baseball Hall of Fame, the first thing that came to mind was not Willie's ability to bunt. To be sure, Willie could definitely bunt, but he hit 661 home runs and might be the best center fielder who ever played the game.

Dorothy was a complex blend of Catholicism and radical direct action. When she stated that she did not want to be called a saint, it could be interpreted as a statement of humility, but, more importantly, she did not want sainthood to blunt her radical critique of our filthy, rotten system. The bishops of New York didn't ask Dorothy to start the *Catholic Worker*; she did so because she thought hospitality and resistance were obligations. She wasn't interested in charity, a word she could "choke over." She was committed to justice. The extra coat in your closet belongs to the person who has no coat. Justice!

In seeking her canonization, many Catholic Workers fear that the bishops might gloss over Dorothy's resistance to war and violence and the systems that cause people to be poor. Dorothy unequivocally resisted World War II and so was branded a traitor by some. As a result, the *Catholic Worker* newspaper lost thousands of subscribers; many CW houses closed as well. She condemned the bombings of Hiroshima and Nagasaki. During the Vietnam War, the CW was known for its pacifism even more than its hospitality. CW became synonymous with draft resistance. And today, Catholic Workers throughout the world follow Dorothy's opposition to the war machine.

Many Catholic Workers houses, including Viva House, have already declared Dorothy Day a saint by acclamation. Formal canonization is not something we seek. Saints are everywhere. We see them on South Mount Street. Some come to the soup kitchen to eat. Some serve. We do not need a costly canonization process replete with certification of miracles and other trappings of canonization. The real miracle is that Catholic Worker houses grew in number after Dorothy's death, and the work goes on. So, by acclamation: Dorothy Day, the patron saint of hospitality and resistance.

Don't Call Me a Saint

Dorothy Day said it best: "Don't call me a saint. I don't want to be dismissed so easily." Unfortunately, the Paulist Pictures' film, *Entertaining Angels*, appears to be the beginning of an institutional process of dismissing Dorothy Day's most vital gift to American culture and to all religious bureaucracies: a deep-rooted spirituality intrinsically bound to the mandates of the Sermon on the Mount.

Her vision was radical. She did not seek what German theologian and war resistor Dietrich Bonhoeffer called "cheap grace." She confronted our welfare/warfare state. The film portrays Dorothy as beginning some sort of helping-up mission. Thus, it avoids the essence of the Catholic Worker philosophy and its critique of this society.

The film ends in 1937 at almost precisely the moment when the Catholic Worker movement came in direct conflict with the U.S. government, American capitalism, and the institutional church.

Ending as it does in 1937, the film never shows Dorothy taking a pacifist stand against World War II or calling President Harry S. Truman to task for the genocidal act of dropping hydrogen bombs on Hiroshima and Nagasaki. The viewer never learns that the Catholic Worker's commitment to pacifism led many to withdraw their support.

The film never shows the fact that Dorothy and several workers were arrested many times for refusing to "take shelter" during the insane air-raid drills of the 1950s. Remember in Catholic elementary schools when the nuns made us hide under our desks and pray the rosary during those mandatory drills of the cold war? The nuns should have told us to join Dorothy in open resistance to the nuclear buildup.

The film makes no attempt to portray Dorothy's role in encouraging Catholic Workers to resist the draft and refuse to go to Vietnam. In this she was in direct opposition to people like New York's Francis Cardinal Spellman, who blessed the troops and the bombing of the Vietnamese people. Dorothy did not stand with the American bishops who supported the war. She was shoulder to shoulder with people like Dave Miller and Tom Cornell of the New York Catholic Worker, who burned their draft cards in open defiance of the law.

In the film we never see Dorothy and the Worker movement closely aligned with the striking gravediggers at Calvary Cemetery in Queens, New York, or with the sit-down strikers in Flint, Michigan, or the United Farm Workers in California, to mention but a few of those seeking workplace justice.

Well, we could go on and on about what is left out of the film. It's like trying to know the body without its spirit, its very soul. It's like making a film about El Salvador, or Salvadoran bishop Oscar Romero and leaving out the struggle of the Salvadoran people.

The woman depicted in Entertaining Angels is not the Dorothy who stayed at Viva House in 1968 during the trial of the Catonsville Nine. She is not the Dorothy who welcomed students from Baltimore's Mercy High School when we visited the New York Worker in 1973. She is not the Dorothy who told all of us clearly and without equivocation that "our problems stem from our acceptance of this filthy rotten system." Dorothy had a structural analysis that was as deep as the core of her spirituality.

Entertaining Angels is the story of some woman's conversion. It might well be a powerful story of a conversion. But it is not about Dorothy Day. It is not the story of this fine woman who knew that resistance to war, violence, and greed were but the opposite side of the coin of hospitality, who knew that "love in action was a harsh and dreadful thing compared to love in dreams." Dorothy knew that her kind of love meant hard but beautiful days in soup kitchens and houses of hospitality. She also knew that it required tough, gruesome, faith-challenging days in and out of kangaroo courts, in and out of jails, day in and day out. A diet of hospitality and resistance.

Dorothy's conversion to Catholicism didn't come out of nowhere. She had a rich social background. She was already a compassionate and politically astute woman. She understood and lived the cry of the Wobblies: "An injury to one is an injury to all."

But this was not enough for her. She was indeed pursued by God, the "hound of heaven." And there was a reason for God's pursuit. She taught many of us for the first time the real mystery of the Eucharist, the mystery of the Mystical Body. Her teaching tools were direct action, a profoundly prayerful and liturgical life and truthful writing. "The mystery of the poor," she said, "is that they are Jesus, and what we do to them we do to Him."

We hoped for more in this film. My God, what a film it could have been.

The
long
loneliness

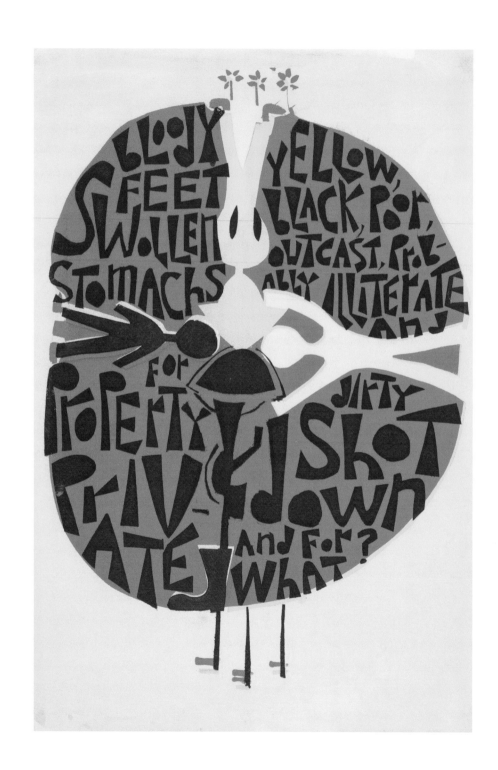

Chapter 7: Conscience

A Burning Incident at Mercy High

September 12, 1973, is a date I well remember. I was co-teaching an interdisciplinary English/theology class at Baltimore's Mercy High School with Sally Swann, a creative and thoughtful English teacher. It was the day after the U.S.-supported military coup in Chile. The Vietnam War was still raging and we were bombing Cambodia, making it an even wider war.

The title of our course was Freedom and Suffering. It was designed around a series of questions: What is freedom? Why do humans suffer? Is anyone free if everyone is not free? If I do not want freedom to be a lie, what risk and suffering is then demanded of me? Sally and I believed that raising such questions brought us face to face with theological concepts of death and rebirth, that is to say resurrection.

September 12 was our first class. We began by explaining three fundamental presuppositions of the course: 1.) The Gospel treats everyone's life with respect. Thus, the course would examine freedom and suffering from the perspective of the fate of the majority of humankind, who suffer hunger, disease, warfare, and violence. 2.) The Gospel message is universal. It mentions no flags and no country, and so in the course no precedence would be given to one county over another. 3.) Jesus took seriously the notion that "a way of liberation passes through fire." And so the course will ask, "How far am I willing to pass through that fire myself?"

This last point especially suggests that fire is a symbol of purification. So, in that first class I burned (in a small trash can; immediately extinguished) five items as a way of representing symbolically, both the Biblical command to rid ourselves of idols and the Gospel paradoxes that you have everything when you have nothing, and that death brings life. I burned a miniature American flag because for many Americans it had become an idol, even as for many non-Americans who have suffered because of this country's enormous wealth, it was a symbol of America's power. I burned an image of Jesus, not to burn Jesus but to purify the church's institutionalization of him, forgetting that he embodied in action what his words said. I burned money, to symbolize its power to make people greedy rather than share with the community. And I burned advertisements for ITT and *Playboy* magazine, the former to say something about the power of corporate wealth over people's lives, the latter to signify sexism and the exploitation of women.

In addition to burning these symbols, we squeezed a bag of non-union grapes to acknowledge the plight of farm workers as well as all workers who are treated like machinery. After these actions, we passed around bread and grape juice to celebrate the spirit of unity. We also talked about nonviolence as a means of attaining freedom. Holding a rock in one hand and an egg in the other, Sally and I said that the rock symbolized decay, apathy, and death and that it had to be broken. Instead of violently smashing the rock with a larger rock, however, we would try to break it with an egg, without breaking the egg. We asked everyone to think about this: it may seem absurd, but there is truth and life in the idea. Class discussion that day was quite lively. And of course students disagreed about the symbolic meaning of the five items I burned.

The most controversial was the American flag. Indeed, in the political storm that followed when word got out, most people thought that the flag was the only symbol we burned. The *Baltimore Sun* and the *News American* newspapers ran articles and even an editorial about it, as if it were a public event rather than a contained, contextualized classroom experience. Television newscasters and one particular right-wing talk show host ranted on for over a week. They did this without ever speaking with me personally, to ask what happened, what our intention was. (To its credit the editors of the News American did subsequently print my explanation of the action and the meaning of the course.)

The Baltimore City police and the FBI visited the school to investigate a possible criminal offense. And to compound the controversy, I had a trial in Washington, D.C. at the end of September. I had been part of the Pray-Ins at the White House. During the month of August, small groups of activists had broken away from White House tours, kneeled down, and began praying for an end to U.S. bombing in Cambodia. Our group was, of course, arrested and found guilty, but as luck would have it, we were only given a few months of unsupervised probation. I only missed one day of class.

I didn't lose my job. Although the parents' club at Mercy wanted me out, the principal, Sr. Barbara Mary, RSM, handled significant backlash with great courage and wisdom. Nor was I prosecuted by the federal or locals courts. I was just portrayed as a teacher who used bad judgment and was wrong. But I lasted only through the year.

However, about half of the original thirty-two students dropped the course either of their own volition or because their parents didn't want their daughters exposed to perceived radical theology/philosophy. I do wish they had stayed with the course. I believe they would have appreciated the content and the questions we explored throughout the semester. I wish everyone could have participated in our field trip to New York City, where we had arranged a visit to the New York Catholic Worker house and had lunch with Dorothy Day. Her autobiography, *The Long Loneliness*, was one of our required readings. But to be quite honest, I am not sure if the students actually knew who Dorothy was or that her revolutionary brand of Catholicism had sunk in. In truth teachers always hope that students actually do the readings and get what teachers want them to get out of a course. I do know that my knowledge of freedom and suffering increased enormously.

Now forty years on very little has changed. Although U.S. troops are not in Vietnam, they are in Afghanistan, preparing for Syria. And before Iraq, we intervened in Chile, Nicaragua, El Salvador, Panama, Grenada, and on and on and on. The world remains awash with blood and unrelenting poverty. I would still teach the same course and still present the same symbols. However, I would not burn any of them. I would discuss fire as a means of purification, but the actual burning turned away too many people and became an obstacle to the intended result. Probably it would have been wiser to stain the flag with red dye, symbolizing blood, and then try to wash it out with soap and water. Besides, I'm quite sure that if I taught the same class today, there would be an indictment. Homeland Security would be sniffing around and terrorism charges considered.

Still, the questions remain: Do we Americans hate life? Can we stop consuming? Can we stop the killing? Who knows? Maybe the course helped a few people consider these questions.

Good Samaritans and Systemic Change

Luke's parable of the Good Samaritan is compelling. We listen to the cry of one person. If we really hear the depth of his cry, we will never be the same again.

The parable is simple. A man is traveling from Jerusalem to Jericho. He is stopped. Beaten. Robbed. Left for dead. He cries out ever so feebly. Two people bypass him. Then a Samaritan, a supposed enemy, stops. Quite simply he hears the cry, sees the blood, and stops. He binds the man's wounds, provides him with shelter and medical attention, and demonstrates the compassion that makes us all feel better about being human.

The Samaritan is lauded in homilies. He is good. Such a charitable man. He truly loves his brother and becomes the epitome of what it means to be a neighbor. Everyone, it seems, can relate to the Samaritan. The state can. So can the institutional church.

When a person shares time, food, clothing, and shelter with someone in need, our society is outwardly pleased. Samaritans are caring people. Indeed, we never want individual acts of compassion to cease, because we believe our neighbor has a claim on us. Jesus says so.

This parable is also complex. Perhaps we should examine it more deeply. Perhaps we should ask why the beating? Why the robbery? Why was a person brutalized and left for dead? Who is responsible?

We know that two individuals bypassed the wounded man. We don't really know why. Let's be generous and hopeful. Let's suppose the individuals who bypassed the man in the ditch were also good people. Let's suppose they had an excellent reason for passing by. Let's suppose they understood who was doing the beating, the robbing, the murdering on Jericho roads all over the globe. And this understanding led them to an equally important form of direct action.

This reading of the parable suggests that, in addition to having compassion for an individual, it is necessary to understand the root cause of the brutality. The systemic cause. If we fail to understand the cause, we will continue to have wounded and murdered people in ditches always and everywhere. If we do not deal with the systemic cause, we will continue to bandage the wounds without finding out who is responsible for the wounds.

It is possible to identify today's robbers and murderers. They are nuclear weapons and nuclear stockpiles. They are stealth planes and MX missiles and a mentality that is disturbed by losing and still wants the U.S. to win the war in Vietnam. They are drone attacks killing the innocent. They are the tax dollars that are flushed down the Pentagon toilet each year. Over half of each U.S. tax dollar goes to the war department and thus is an act of larceny against those who lack human necessities.

Neither the state nor the church really wants us to understand systemic problems. It is easier to treat the victims, to provide money, counseling, food, clothing, and shelter. But when people address systemic issues, when they urge nonviolent resistance to the status quo, the church is often silent. In reality we must urge people to refuse to pay taxes that support war. We should have urged them to burn their draft cards and not cooperate with those who make murder legitimate.

The Good Samaritan is the one who stops and helps an individual. But let's remember there is more to it than that. The Good Samaritan is also the person who says no with body and soul. The Good Samaritan understands that justice is connected with personal risk.

Our church should urge us to be real Samaritans. In any election year, voting usually changes nothing. As Phil Berrigan used to say, "If voting could change the system, it would be illegal."

No, the real choice every year is to vote against war. Vote to dismantle the nuclear arsenal. Vote to make plowshares out of swords. Vote to confront the robbers and murderers in a nonviolent way. This kind of voting can only be done with one's physical presence, taking into account all the physical and spiritual risks.

Vote against the system that leaves people beaten, robbed, left for dead. Bandage the wounded. Absolutely. And always remember as an anonymous sage put it, "When they come for the innocent without crossing over your body, cursed be your religion and your life."

We Drink from the Common Cup

No matter how corrupt the Church may become, it carries within itself the seeds of its own regeneration. As a convert, I never expected much from the bishops. In all history, popes and bishops and father abbots seem to have been blind and power hungry and greedy. I never expected leadership from them. It is the saints who keep appearing all through history, who keep things going.
—Dorothy Day

It seems the older I get, the more reflective I become. I tend to move slower but think deeper.

My wife, Willa, and I are both in our seventies now. For almost half a century, we have been with Viva House. We now have a clear understanding of what it means to do the works of mercy and resist the works of war. It seems we have done little to change the world or the city of Baltimore or even our own neighborhood, but we believe that the world hasn't changed us either, which is something positive.

Meanwhile, the soup pots and cases of canned goods feel heavier, while the lines for the kitchen and pantry seem endless. At one time Viva House served mostly older men with drug or drinking problems; now we see young families with children.

The house is a place of love in action, which is often "harsh and dreadful," as Dostoevsky would say, yet it trumps any other way of living. We have tried to be faithful to Dorothy Day's understanding of the need "to bring beauty into the midst of ugliness." Because she believed that "beauty honors and glorifies God. To see such beauty from the dung heap of a slum."

Our lives have roots in the church—baptism, Eucharist, schooling, convent, and seminary. Sometimes, the institutional church reflected beauty and truth, but increasingly, the blind power and greed of the hierarchy tarnishes and even buries both.

The institutional church is in schism. It's breaking apart. The issues are serious. They include issues of social justice, including an overriding complicity of silence about wars in Afghanistan and Iraq, extraordinary rendition, the detention camp at Guantanamo Bay, drone attacks, and the dismantling of social programs that support the common good; gender and economic inequality; and the concentration of power at the top of an all-male hierarchy.

People see the wisdom of H. L. Mencken's comment that "an archbishop is a Christian ecclesiastic of a rank superior to that attained by Christ." Clearly many of those who once occupied the pews have had it with clerical pomposity, aloofness, empty homilies, and hypocrisy.

Additionally, more and more Catholics are appalled at the institution's blatant maltreatment and contempt for U.S. women religious and for our LGBTQ sisters and brothers. The core of the Gospel is clear: We are all one, member for member. There is no justification for dividing people against each other because of gender, race, sexual preference, or country of origin. Anyone who preaches or teaches these hatreds violates the two great commandments to love God and demonstrate that love with our neighbors every day.

My Aunt Kitty was a Dominican nun of unquestionable integrity and insight. She was also a guardian of correct usage of the English language. My sister, Pat, has been a Sister of Charity in New York City since her high school days. She taught elementary school students for decades and still serves her community today. So, for me, the church's attack on the nuns is personal. My aunt and sister worked in the vineyard for years and years. They didn't accumulate property, wear a miter, or have anyone kiss their ring. They just did the work. For many Catholics, the sisters introduced us to social justice and the great commandment of love.

U.S. cardinals and bishops have the gall to call out the nuns and laity over issues like abortion and birth control, even as many of them have been hiding real evil. Between 1950 and 2002, there were more than four thousand reported incidents of priests sexually abusing children. Thus far, U.S. dioceses have paid out well over one billion dollars in abuse lawsuits. These abuses are immoral and criminal. Repentance is needed and apologies aplenty. And a redress of grievances. To paraphrase a quote from an episode of *The Wire*: It seems as if the bishops would rather live in a garbage dump than let the world see them work a shovel.

We agree with Dorothy Day that the church, no matter how corrupt it becomes, "carries within itself the seeds of its own regeneration. . . . It is the saints who keep appearing all through history who keep things going."

Dorothy believed that saints should open their hearts and arms to everyone. They reject worldly power and the accumulation of property and wealth. They abandon the use of violence and say so, even when it means enduring terrible suffering.

In the end, we still have the Sermon on the Mount, community, and the opportunity to practice the command to love one another. We still believe that even when two or three people gather together in the search for community, there is the presence of God. That's what it's all about.

Epilogue

Decades ago, I read Philip Slater's book, *The Pursuit of Loneliness*. He argued that the driving force for citizens of the U.S. was the accumulation of wealth. Not community.

Not interdependence. Not healthcare, education, housing, or full employment. Not even sharing excess with those begging for necessities. He believed that the pursuit of wealth would eventually lead to a state of loneliness for both the haves and have nots. We would become a divided nation.

We are talking about a country where a small fraction of our population lives in luxury while many of our citizens become more impoverished each day. The poorest of the poor are then termed vagrant, beggar, bum. If a person possesses nothing, it's easy to believe that that person is nothing. That person becomes isolated and disconnected from society. That person is alone, and, as Mother Teresa exclaims, "Being alone is the most terrible poverty." Throughout the decades, the Viva House community always approached each day "little by little." We never kidded ourselves about the magnitude of the struggle before us, and we tried not to take ourselves too seriously. We tried to be joyful and ease the loneliness of so many of our neighbors.

Loneliness, we believe, is connected to poverty and violence. They are spokes on the same grinding wheel. Emma Goldman would say it's organized violence at the top that creates individualized violence in our neighborhoods. If you want to understand why a Baltimore teenager shoots another teenager for a few vials of crack, visit the Pentagon. Visit the military sites that conduct drone warfare. A drone expert unleashes bombs on another country, killing people, most of them innocent civilians, with impunity while sipping a cup of morning coffee. Then she or he goes home for dinner.

We have to connect all the dots. The teenager who kills a brother in a dispute over a bag of drugs is as isolated and lonely as the drone expert who kills on Pentagon orders. We don't have meaningful work for the teenager or the drone expert. The teenager sells drugs because that is the only way he can earn a decent income in Sowebo. Increasingly, those who become drone experts have joined the so-called all volunteer army because work that enhances the human community is harder to find. A harsh side effect is that the drone expert teaches the teenager that ultimate violence solves problems.

Rapidly advancing technology is taking away jobs from millions of workers.

Manufacturing jobs keep decreasing, and creating more public sector jobs that serve the common good is met with public resistance. We have come face to face with the reality of expendable labor. Too many people have lost their jobs and are forced to stand alone. This is a recipe for disaster, and it is a global problem affecting everyone on the planet.

Dorothy Day has the solution for loneliness, poverty, and violence. It is love, and it can only come with community. We have tried to be such a community in Baltimore, and, as Brian Smeaton, our friend from Belfast, would say, we did the best we could with the information we had during this half century. The "best we could" means paying attention to the wisdom of Vincent de Paul: "It is not enough to give soup and bread. It is only for your love alone that the poor will forgive you the bread you give them."

I have a small grain of **HOPE** —
I need more.

I break off a
fragment to
send you.

Please take this
grain of a grain
of
HOPE
so that mine
won't shrink.

Please **share**
your fragment
so that yours
will
GROW

Only so,
by division,
will
HOPE
increase...

Denise Levertov

12/45 Sheila + Kate

Blessed   are   those

who hunger   and thirst for Justice,

the Justice of God
will be theirs.

104

Acknowledgements

Our book would never have developed without the encouragement, the organizational skills, and the computer wizardry of our daughter, Kate, and our good friend, Rick Connor. They remained committed to the book for an entire year and guided us over many hurdles. We have been blessed.

We also thank Kate and her daughters Grace and Maya Walsh-Little for typing, proofing, and revising page after page. We relied on their clarity and focus. We also appreciate Julia Walsh-Little's keen eye for color and design as she helped us visualize the placement of the art with the text. We can never forget that Dave Walsh-Little took on many, many house chores so that the work on the book could progress.

We are also indebted to John Wheeler and Betsy Wilmerding for reading the text and giving important critical assessments. Our friend Linda Shopes did an astounding job editing the entire manuscript. She understood our work at Viva House and knew what we were trying to express. With a masterful grasp of language, grammar, and style she edited the book and made it into a book we are proud to publish. Linda is an editor whose skill is only exceeded by her tireless attention to detail.

Brendan Walsh

I thank the Sisters of Charity of New York for teaching me how to read. I thank the Jesuits at Fordham Prep for teaching me how to write and study. I thank the English and theology departments at LeMoyne College for showing me how to read critically. I am most thankful to Father Daniel Berrigan, S.J. for introducing me to the real meaning of the Gospel. In fact, Dan's classes were the first time in my life I actually heard the Gospel preached.

I am forever indebted to all the saints I meet each day in Sowebo— the homeless, the struggling families, those searching for work, those battling addiction. They teach me daily what is truly important in this life: we are all part of the same family.

Finally, I will always remember the first five people I met in Baltimore when I arrived in 1967. Phil Berrigan, Jim Harney, Tom Lewis, and Bill and Marilyn O'Connor greeted me warmly and educated me about Vietnam, justice, nonviolence, and the common good. I will always value their friendship and the quality of their lives. They helped Willa and me create this book.

We are most grateful to the students, faculty and staff of Loyola University Maryland for the magnificent support of our food pantry over many decades. And have been encouraged by the students who have worked with us.

And, finally thanks to Kevin Atticks. He realized that we were novices in the computer age and skillfully helped us develop a meaningful piece of work.

Willa Bickham

Art has always been an important part of the Catholic Worker. I thank the many artists that I have studied and worked with over the past fifty years. They include Richard Mehren, CSJ, Barrie Barrett, Tom Lewis, Marilyn O'Connor, Mary Jacque Benner, RSM, Joanne Manzo, Jeanne Fischer, Marshal Kinsley, Liz McAlister, Ann Recknor, Bernice Mennis, and David Cunningham. It is important to me that Liz McAlister and I continue to paint together each week.

In addition to working hard on the manuscript with her father, our daughter, Kate Walsh-Little, also did many paintings with me. Indeed her whole family, Dave, Maya, Grace and Julia, do many textiles, murals, silk screen prints, and watercolor paintings with me.

Dorothy Day told us to look for beauty even in the squalor of the streets. She loved Dostoevsky's idea that "the world will be saved by beauty." These words are on one of the murals we painted on the side wall of Viva House. The beauty and tragedy of sharing a lifetime with our West Baltimore neighbors inspire all the art work we do. The works of mercy and the works of resistance are the themes of my work.

I also want to say how supportive my brother, Paul Bickham of St. Louis, and sisters, Sheila Moore and Carey Cunniffe of Chicago, and their families have been.

Bibliography

Baker, Kimball. *"Go to the Worker"*: America's Labor Apostles. Milwaukee: Marquette University Press, 2010.

Berrigan, Philip. *No More Strangers*. New York: Macmillan, 1965.

Consedine, Jim. *Restorative Justice: Healing the Effects of Crime*. Lyttelton, NZ: Ploughshares Publications, 1995.

Day, Dorothy. *The Long Loneliness: The Autobiography of Dorothy Day*. San Francisco: Harper & Row, 1981.

Fisher, James Terence. *On the Irish Waterfront: The Crusader, the Movie, and the Soul of the Port of New York*. Ithaca: Cornell University Press, 2009.

Gandhi, M.K. *Nonviolent Resistance*. New York: Schocken Books, 1961.

Hodgson, Godfrey. *The Myth of American Exceptionalism*. New Haven: Yale University Press, 2009.

The Jerusalem Bible. Garden City, NY: Doubleday, 1966.

Kozol, Jonathan. *Savage Inequalities: Children in America's Schools*. New York: Crown Publishing Group, 1991.

Lee, Spike. *When the Levees Broke: A Requiem in Four Acts*. Film. Directed by Spike Lee. New York: Home Box Office, 2006.

Leo XIII, *Rerum Novarum* (Revolutionary Change): *On the Condition of the Working Class*. Encyclical Letter. Vatican City: Vatican Publishing House, *1891*.

Maurin, Peter. *Easy Essays*. Steubenville, OH: Franciscan University Press, 1977.

Merton, Thomas. *Raids on the Unspeakable*. New York: New Directions, 1966.

Myers, Ched. *Binding the Strong Man: A Political Reading of Mark's Story of Jesus*. Maryknoll, NY: Orbis, 1988.

Perrin, Henri. *Priest and Worker: The Autobiography of Henri Perrin*. New York: Holt, Rinehart and Winston,

1964.

Simon, David and Edward Burns. *The Corner: A Year in the Life of an Inner-City Neighborhood.* New York: Broadway Book, 1997.

Zinn, Howard. *A People's History of the United States.* New York: Harper & Row, 1980. _____. *You Can't Be Neutral on a Moving Train: A Personal History of Our Times.* Boston: Beacon Press, 1994.

Broadway, 1997.PrintZinn, Howard. *A People's History of the United States.* New York: Harper & Row, 1980. Print.

Zinn, Howard. *You Can't Be Neutral on a Moving Train: A Personal History of Our Times.* Boston: Beacon, 1994. Print.

Rerum Novarum by Pope Leo XIII

The Jerusalem Bible. Garden City, NY: Doubleday, 1966. Print

Apprentice House is the country's only campus-based, student-staffed book publishing company. Directed by professors and industry professionals, it is a nonprofit activity of the Communication Department at Loyola University Maryland.

Using state-of-the-art technology and an experiential learning model of education, Apprentice House publishes books in untraditional ways. This dual responsibility as publishers and educators creates an unprecedented collaborative environment among faculty and students, while teaching tomorrow's editors, designers, and marketers.

Outside of class, progress on book projects is carried forth by the AH Book Publishing Club, a co-curricular campus organization supported by Loyola University Maryland's Office of Student Activities.

Eclectic and provocative, Apprentice House titles intend to entertain as well as spark dialogue on a variety of topics. Financial contributions to sustain the press's work are welcomed. Contributions are tax deductible to the fullest extent allowed by the IRS.

To learn more about Apprentice House books or to obtain submission guidelines, please visit www.apprenticehouse.com.

Apprentice House
Communication Department
Loyola University Maryland
4501 N. Charles Street
Baltimore, MD 21210
Ph: 410-617-5265 • Fax: 410-617-2198
info@apprenticehouse.com • www.apprenticehouse.com

CPSIA information can be obtained at www.ICGtesting.com
Printed in the USA
BVIW12n0843090916
461620BV00002B/2